Overcoming Challenge:
The Tar-Billy Way

Ernest Hamilton

POCAHONTAS PRESS

DUBLIN, VA

Overcoming Challenge:
The Tar-Billy Way

ISBN 13: 978-1-955338-05-9

Cover design by Ernest Hamilton
Interior design by Deborah Warren
Printed in the United States of America

PP

POCAHONTAS PRESS

DUBLIN, VA
POCAHONTASPRESS.COM

Dedicated to Julie, Cody, Eason and Haven

Throughout this book, I talk about many people who have had a positive influence on me. There are so many people I have been blessed to have in my life. However, four specific people have inspired me more than anyone. Julie, Cody, Eason, and Haven, you have been the backbone of much of my motivation. Nothing is more important to me than modeling for you that anything is possible. Throughout my career, you've had to settle for second place many times so I could accomplish my goals. I've missed birthdays, ball games, family gatherings, and more. Through it all, it hasn't been easy and even hard at times to understand why I had to go out of town for work, take business calls at home, or miss one of your special days.

My desire all along was to make a positive impact in my workplace and among my colleagues, but I've especially wanted to inspire you. I want you to know that the sky's the limit! You are bound to make mistakes, but I encourage you to learn from them. You will encounter challenges, and I urge you to face them head on. I have no doubt that you will accomplish goals that you might never think are possible. No matter where your goals and dreams take you, always know that I love you.

Contents

1

Just to Get You Thinking

Have you ever thought about how different your life has turned out from what you'd originally planned? When you're young, you dream about what you want to do with your life and you may even have a plan for how to accomplish your goal. Growing older, many people find that life turned out much differently than they expected. When I was young, all I wanted to do was drive a truck, and I could never picture myself doing anything else. My life has taken twists and turns, involving me in things I never thought I'd be a part of. Now that I am older, I've come to realize how rewarding my life has turned out to be, though not because of hard times or good luck, but because of friendship, teamwork, a great family, and most importantly, the fear of failing.

The weird thing about life is the fact that when we are born, we are a clean slate, able to become whomever we want or do anything we want with our lives. Our future has yet to be written, giving us the flexibility to write our own story. I know a lot of people say that this isn't possible because of the financial struggles some are born into, but I don't believe that's true. In this day and age, there are numerous government programs available to aid people in getting a college education or even a job. These programs can help you overcome the financial obstacles in your path, but it's up to you to decide to take advantage of the programs and make good use of them. You don't have to be smart, rich, or popular, just willing to use whatever talent God has blessed you with and be persistent.

A sad fact is that many people don't take full advantage of the opportunities that are available to them, or they abuse the system, causing hard working people to have to struggle even more. Some folks sit around making up excuses as to why they can't do any better, and, in many cases, blame others for their lifestyle. Truth is, there are two different ways to look at challenges. You can look at every challenge as though it is a setback keeping you from achieving your goal, and give up. Or you can look at each challenge as an opportunity to learn, grow, and go further than you dreamed.

Challenges and frustrations are some of the hardest things to deal with in life because it seems that when one thing goes wrong, five more follow it. However, when you think about it, most people who have become wealthy as a result of their own hard work had to deal with setbacks just like anyone else. The difference is they learned how to view setbacks as growing experiences and moved on. They didn't sit around placing blame on others or waiting for someone else to resolve their issues; they stepped up to the plate, took control of their life, dealt with obstacles, and carried on with their life.

This concept applies to those who choose to follow dreams that will give them a feeling of accomplishment. Our dreams allow us to have purpose. It can be something as simple as finishing school or as complicated as building your career. Either way, you have succeeded, and you are just as successful as the richest man in the world, because you followed your dreams and overcame frustrations to get that feeling of success. Many people associate success with wealth, but remember, being successful doesn't necessarily mean you have a lot of money. In my opinion, it is how you feel in your heart that makes you rich.

One of the most important things you need to do is set your mind on what you want out of life. Once your mind is made up, you'll begin to make decisions based on that goal. In other words, your goal will guide your decision-making process. There are all kinds of examples, but let's use something simple. Remember when you were growing up and you were in school? For most people, graduating and moving on to the next step in life was of utmost importance. No matter whether you liked or didn't like school, you knew there were certain classes you had to pass to graduate. Once you made your mind up you had to pass each course, the decisions you made from that point on guided you toward graduation. Before you knew it, you were graduating and your whole time as a student almost seemed like a blur.

Did you ever stop to wonder why things worked out like that? Did you think it was just fate at work? Truth is, your mind led you to that point in your life. Your mind set a goal once you decided you wanted to graduate. From that point on, every decision you made was your mind trying to reach that special day. Your mind subconsciously guided you toward paying more attention in class, getting your homework done properly and turned in on time, asking questions if you didn't quite understand the material, and spending less time with friends and more time studying.

It's no different when you get older, though you'll be dealing with things much bigger than high school. You'll begin thinking about life-where you want to be, who you want to be, and how you're going to get there. You set goals and your plan is to not let anyone stand in your way, which brings me to my next point.

What role do other people play in your success? Should you listen to every piece of advice an adult gives you? Do you listen to children? What about the professionals in the field you want to go into? Do you listen to each one of them? Well, the simple answer is yes, you need to listen to everyone. Yet, that doesn't mean you should take every piece of advice. I would caution against taking any advice until you've had time to think about it. You're sure to use all the information ingrained in the advice you have been given, but you may use it in a different way than it was originally intended. Now that you are confused, let me try to explain.

Say you work with two people. Jack is smart, easy to get along with, has historically offered good advice, and knows the job well. He has worked at the job much longer than you. He doesn't always know the right answer, but most of the time he does. You both know that if a wrong decision is made, your boss will be upset with you. To avoid upsetting your boss, do you go along with every idea Jack has just because he's been at the job longer and is usually right about things? Or do you think through situations yourself, considering what needs to be done, and offer suggestions to Jack about how things could be done differently when the situation seems to warrant it? I think you'd want to make the right decision and stay on your boss's good side, so you talk through things, learn from Jack's experience, and get the job done the right way.

Jill, on the other hand, is just the opposite of Jack. Jill frequently does things wrong, doesn't get along well with others, offers bad advice quite often, and gets very upset when you or another coworker gets a pat on the back from the boss. Now, you may be wondering, "How could I use any information from Jill?" The answer is simple. Pay close attention to what Jill does so you don't make the same mistakes. At the same time, don't assume that all Jill's actions are going to be mistakes. Jill might make some good decisions from time to time that you could learn from as well.

Jill may also offer some bad advice at times. Now, how in the world do you learn from bad advice? Advice is all about passing on what one person has learned to someone else so that the same mistake isn't made twice. If you listen to five different pieces of advice from five different people, then you will have a greater understanding of the issue than before. By listening and educating yourself, you'll be able to use the good advice to your advantage and know what the right move is. You'll use bad advice to avoid making as many mistakes.

Most people who give us advice are only trying to help us, which means they care to some extent about the decisions we make. Those decisions could be ones that will affect only us, or they could be decisions that also affect the advice giver's interest. Think about all the people who have given you advice over the years. For most of us, this began with our parents and grandparents, who were always trying to steer us in the right direction. The advice didn't cost us anything and usually had a drastic effect on the decisions we made and how our lives turned out.

My personal life was tremendously affected by my family. It all started with being a part of a great family. No matter what I've attempted in my life, they've been there to support me. This includes everyone in my family, not just my parents. Now, don't get me wrong, our family has our share of problems like all families do, but we still stick together and look after one another. This includes all areas of life like working on trucks, cooking, remodeling someone's house, taking care of elderly family members, and even working on a farm. When I was young, I didn't think much about these things, but now that I'm older, I treasure those times. They taught me a lot about being a team player, hard work, and never giving up no matter what happens. Although this support growing up was always there, it was never more obvious to me than when I was in my twenties and thirties.

2

Overview of My Younger Years

My birthday is on October 31, yes, Halloween. As I said in chapter 1, I came from a good home, not a perfect one. We had our share of problems, but no more than most families. We weren't rich, but we weren't living on the streets either. My parents worked hard to provide enough for us to live on and have a few extra things. I can remember when work was good and when work was slow and my parents worried about how we were going to eat. I'm not ashamed of how I grew up. In fact, I'm very proud of the struggles we went through because they taught me that hard work is a necessity; to never give up, no matter what; and that if you want something bad enough, you can get it.

I was a typical country boy growing up. I liked trucks, cars, playing in the dirt, and of course getting into my share of mischief from time to time. Like most other kids, I liked to dream about life, and I was fortunate enough to have experiences that allowed me to be involved in many things that other kids didn't get to do. I was allowed to go to work with my dad if I was out of school. I was able to go on hunting trips with my grandpa for a week at a time. I was involved in big projects like building and working on things. Growing up those things didn't seem important, but as I've gotten older, these are things in my life that I cherish. I learned a tremendous amount about life's rewards and struggles, because all of the adults involved in these projects or adventures were caring adults that set a good example for me.

I was and still am a person that doesn't mind stepping away from the crowd and being myself. I noticed many young people then, and even now, would agree with their peers just to fit in, but I've never done that. Don't get me wrong, I've done things with my peers I shouldn't have, but because I, myself, chose to do so, not because I was trying to fit in. For this reason, I've gotten to experience being an outcast as well as somewhat popular. However, no matter my social status, I don't remember ever giving in or agreeing with someone just to be part of the crowd. My view has always been that I'm going to be myself and don't care what people think about me, as long as I'm honest with myself.

In fact, I'd say that being both popular and unpopular at different times in my life has taught me the value of friendship. From those that didn't like me, I learned I didn't want to treat other people the way they had treated me. On the other hand, from those who respected my opinion I learned how good it felt to be able to be myself and how I wanted other people to feel around me. You see in movies and TV shows so many young people being bullied and ridiculed. These shows send the message that those being bullied are suffering more than those who are actually doing the bullying, but there's another way to look at it. In the long run, I think those doing the bullying come out on the losing end, because they don't learn the true value of friendship. The decisions they've made will lead them down a lonely road if they don't change their ways. Eventually, the person being bullied will get away from the bully and will know the true meaning of friendship, which will make them a much better person in life.

The first fifteen years of my life were spent in Tazewell, Virginia. For me, it was a wonderful place to grow up. It's a small town in southwestern Virginia populated with middle-class hardworking people. It's amazing some of the things I can remember about growing up in this town. For example, I remember that crime was almost nonexistent. When you left the house, you didn't worry about locking the doors to your house. In my childhood I only remember one violent crime taking place, when a man shot his wife, daughter, and then himself. Other than that, it was a town where it seemed nothing exciting ever took place. Everyone seemed to know most everyone else in town, and your word was as good as any contract in today's world.

I can remember there being four almost perfect seasons. Summer was hot during the day, but cool at night. Air conditioning was just becoming popular, but many of the older people wouldn't even consider having it. In fact, I can remember not having air conditioning in our house for a few years. Fall was generally gorgeous with the leaves changing, and the temperatures would remain decent for a couple months. The tree-covered mountains provided a spectacular view during fall. Many people still used wood/coal burning stoves and spent this time preparing for the bad weather that was to come. Winter was usually cold with plenty of snow that was pretty to watch against the mountainous landscape. In fact, watching it snow is one of the most beautiful sights to observe, in my opinion. It is one thing I don't think I'll ever grow tired of seeing. To this day, I would rather watch it snow than eat. Spring days were warm, but mornings and nights were still cold. The trees blooming on the mountainside was a spectacular sight.

Up until February of 1990, my mom worked as a teller at a bank and my dad owned a truck, which he used to haul coal in the mountains of West Virginia. Most of the time, for all I knew we did alright financially. However, thinking back, I do recall noticing some times when things got rough. Owning his own truck and operating it for the coal business meant that Dad's income was affected when the coal mines were not busy. But, just because work fell off, that didn't mean the truck and house payment weren't still due. On top of that, we still had to eat. Regardless, Mom always made sure we had clothes on our backs, food in our bellies, and anything else we needed. Dad made sure we had a roof over our heads. Together, they both made sure we had enough money to afford to live.

I come from a huge family that's spread out over numerous states. I remember each year we'd have a family reunion at the park in Tazewell, and family members would travel from Ohio, Vermont, West Virginia, North Carolina, Maryland, and Kentucky to attend. I don't remember exactly how many would show up each year, but I'm guessing 150 or better most years. My great-grandmother would spend an entire year organizing everything, and everyone made a point to come every year. I guess everyone enjoyed the reunions as much as I did.

My great-grandmother had a big influence on me growing up. I never heard her say anything bad or even remotely negative about another person. I've seen her get quiet and maybe give the impression she didn't agree with something, but she wouldn't comment on it. In fact, I never heard anything negative come out of her mouth at all. In the late 1980s, she got sick for the first time that I can remember in her life. She was in her late eighties at the time. My great-grandfather had already passed on, which meant she was living alone. After she got sick, she wanted someone to stay with her. She didn't need them to really do anything, just to be there in case she fell or became ill so they could call for help. I was about thirteen or fourteen at the time and somehow, I ended up staying with her for about six months. There wasn't a lot for a young boy to do at her house, and I would get bored. Looking back, though, I really enjoyed staying with her. I remember her telling me stories of things that had happened in her life and how vividly she could tell those stories. Every morning she would wake me for school by saying "Ern, it's time to get up for school." She was adamant that I eat breakfast before school every day, even though eating breakfast is something that didn't agree with me so early in the morning. Her favorite shows were *Good Morning America, Nashville Now with Ralph Emery,* and *The Cosby Show*. I especially remember *The Cosby Show* because we would watch it together every Thursday night at eight o'clock. Other than those three shows, she didn't watch television.

I remember our family gathering at Grandmother's house on Sundays to eat dinner. She and some of the other women in my family would cook up a meal so good it still makes my mouth water to think about it. After dinner, there was no jumping up and washing the dishes immediately. Instead, we'd cover the food with a sheet, then go out on the porch to spend time with the family. Usually, the adults would stay on the porch while the kids played in the yard. No matter if it was on the porch or at the park, that time with my family is something that will always be cherished.

When I was around seven or eight years old, my dad was working in Phelps, Kentucky hauling coal. He'd be gone a week at a time, only coming home on the weekends. During this time, my younger sister and I had our two half-sisters on my mom's side living with us. This left me as the only boy at home among four females. Momma always took good care of us, making sure we were decent for school, that we ate when we came home, and that we were in bed at a reasonable hour.

She'd read us a book at night, take care of us when we got hurt, and tear our tail up if we got out of line. Although I love my momma very much, I sure looked forward to my dad coming home on the weekends. After being alone with that many females for a week in one house, I was ready to do some boy stuff. Being so young at the time, I wasn't allowed to go off and do things on my own. When my dad was gone, I was stuck with the girls, whether I liked it or not.

On weekends when Dad was home, he'd let me tag along with him wherever he went. Most times on Saturday, we gathered up truck parts and ran errands he had gotten behind on while he'd been gone. Then sometimes on Sunday, he'd take me to get ice cream in town. We'd both get a vanilla cone, but he would have to help me with mine because I couldn't eat it fast enough to keep it from melting. Other times he would take me camping, fishing, or riding four wheelers in the mountains of West Virginia. It didn't matter where we went or what we did, I loved it when I was with my dad.

My grandpa (my dad's father) was a man of great wisdom, in my opinion. He could fix most anything. His philosophy was if you can't fix it, stop trying to fix it and figure out how it works. Then you'll be able to fix it. Both of my grandmothers were always cooking and taking me places. My uncles drove trucks and operated equipment. They liked to go have fun on the weekends if they weren't doing maintenance on equipment, which happened a lot. I remember all of these people telling me stories and just spending time with me. We didn't have to be on the go all the time. Sometimes hanging out in the yard at home watching the trees sway in the breeze and talking was enough entertainment for us. In fact, many days I still consider it quality entertainment.

Times were so much simpler in those days. Everyone tried to look after one another. And not just in my family.

It seemed like it was in everyone's nature to help their fellow man. I remember going down to my great Uncle Buster's farm and helping cut silage. My dad would drive Uncle Buster's farm truck alongside the tractor to load it. Then he'd go to the bin to dump, and return to get another load. Most of the time I would ride with my dad, but sometimes I'd go find my cousin Michael, who was the same age as me, and we would go play in the woods or walk down to the creek. I recall many times growing up people pulling together to help one another. It was always pretty evenly split. Sometimes my family would be helping someone else, and other times, they would be helping us.

Experiencing and seeing this firsthand, may be why it's in my nature to help other folks. The biggest job we ever accomplished together was moving a doublewide home down a mountain with a bulldozer, backwards. My Uncle Junior had purchased the home, which was sitting on top of the mountain. He lived halfway down the same mountain. I didn't go the first two days to help, but I had good reason. Some new neighbors had moved in up the street from us. One had pretty, blonde hair (which I liked), one was a redhead, and the other was a brunette. I didn't know their names yet, but my cousins and I were trying to find out. We'd go walking in the neighborhood hoping to see them. There was really no point though, because at that age, none of us had enough nerve to talk to them. Still, we went many times every day.

Daddy came home at the end of the second day and asked me if I would go help with the doublewide move on the third day. I told him I didn't want to go, but I couldn't tell him why. It was too embarrassing. I was thirteen years old, and up to this point, girls had been a bad thing. I knew if I told Daddy I would rather chase girls than go help him, he would pick at me. Nevertheless, he wanted me to go. He even sweetened the pot by telling me I could drive the pick-up truck and run block for them. For a boy of thirteen, a chance to drive outweighed chasing a girl any day, no matter how pretty and blonde her hair was. So I went.

We arrived at about 6:30 a.m. My uncle was staying in a camper on the property until we got his new home moved in. We sat around the camper for about 30 minutes and finally ventured off to the top of the mountain where the home had been parked the day before. When we arrived, I noticed they had hooked the home to a bulldozer instead of a truck. I can remember thinking to myself, "This is going to be interesting." I also noticed that there were people showing up from every direction. I could not figure out what all of these people were going to do. However, I soon found out.

The first thing they did was put two people on top of the home. Their job was to cut any tree limbs that would hit the house and cause damage. Between the two of them, they had chain saws and other tools they might need. There were about three people on each side of the home to serve as guides. If any one of them saw anything that would damage the home, they were to holler to the front so the driver of the dozer (which happened to be my uncle) could be stopped or guided in another direction.

The most important person on the team was my grandpa because he was the main guide. He walked backwards behind the dozer taking his directions from those staged around the home. Once he got direction from them, he would combine the information and relay it to my uncle on the dozer. Keep in mind, this was being done on a one-lane dirt road that looked like it was laid out by a black snake, with all the curves and switchbacks it had in it. The home was so wide, it took up the whole road in the couple of straight stretches and both ditch lines in all the curves. Nevertheless, they worked at it for two days to move the home about two miles. Not only was it a very slow process, it was one of the most impressive displays of teamwork that I have ever witnessed, and I am so glad I was there to see it. Little did I know, this project and various others I was a part of growing up, set the stage for other accomplishments in my life.

In the latter part of 1989, the coal industry fell and jobs became scarce. My dad got hooked up with a man by the name of Jeff Hagy in North Carolina, through a friend. Next thing I knew, the coal truck was being modified and taken to North Carolina to help build roads and other various projects. Jeff allowed my dad to stay with him until he got on his feet. I'm very thankful for Jeff to this day. In February of 1990, my family and I moved to Dunn, N.C. to join my dad.

Living in North Carolina was fun at first. I made many friends and learned a lot about a different culture. It wasn't long after we moved that I had my sixteenth birthday. My parents had a 1983 Chevrolet Cavalier they let me drive. It was in fair shape, but would nickel and dime you to death with little things needing repair. At any rate, it got me where I wanted to go. In February of 1991, I got a job with a local grocery store as a bagger. I remember my dad telling me if I got in my mind that I wanted a newer vehicle, I would have to show him I could save some money up first. It wasn't long before I'd done just that and was begging for a new Chevrolet S-10 pickup.

It took a bit of convincing, but he finally decided to sign the papers for me. I'll never forget what he told me when he handed me the keys for the first time. He said, "If the payment isn't in my hand each month, the keys will be." I worked my butt off at Carlie C's IGA grocery store to make those payments each month, which was tough at four and five dollars an hour. I would work every time the store needed me, and I even stopped by to see if they needed me when I was off. Of course, once they learned I was willing to work, they'd call me if someone else didn't show up for a shift. I worked every minute I could. There were many times when my friends would be going to do something fun, and I was headed to work.

This is probably one of the best things that ever happened to me, because working kept me out of trouble. I finally paid that truck off, and I was so proud because it was mine and I earned it. It was not a full-size truck like many of my friends had, but the fact I had paid for it on my own was so rewarding. I learned the value of a dollar, work ethic, and that you can do anything you set your mind to. I also learned that you have to make sacrifices in order to reap the rewards.

3

Starting at Food Lion

On April 9, 1993, I began a job at a Food Lion Distribution Center in Dunn, North Carolina. I was eighteen years old and began as a selector, someone who selects the product that the stores have ordered. The warehouse was mapped out like a giant grocery store where everything had its own slot, but the products were in cases, not individual packages like they are in the stores we shop in every day. My job was to take a specific store's order which I had been assigned, go by each slot, stack the product on a pallet, and then take the pallet to a loading door. Here, a loader would load the pallet onto a trailer to go to the store, and I would go fill another order.

What sounds easy turned out to be a hard job, a very hard job. The production quota on this job was 300 cases an hour, and every hour counted toward an end of the week average. It didn't matter if you were sick, tired, or what; production still stood. There was no time to stop to socialize or kill time, you had to work to meet quota. Nevertheless, it paid good money. Here I was, an eighteen-year-old boy making $35,000 a year with only a high school diploma. This was much better than what I had made at my previous job, and I was not about to let it go. I made up my mind that I was tougher than the job. Food Lion also had good benefits and an opportunity to grow.

Another reason I stuck with this job was that I wanted to drive a truck for Food Lion. My dad had talked to some of the drivers during his travels and had been told that it was one of the best truck driving jobs there is. Drivers were home every night, were paid by the hour, and were not overworked as compared to other truck drivers in the industry.

The man who hired me as a selector told me that if I worked hard, kept my record clean, and worked every day I was scheduled, that in a year or two I could change positions to something that was better suited for me. I stuck it out for a year and the more I worked at the job the easier it got. Eventually, I got to where I could pull 450 cases an hour in boxed meat, which was good for that department, because the boxes were bigger and heavier. The hardest part of the entire job was being on third shift. This was a job where you had to feel good when you came to work because it was all physical. It wasn't too bad from the second night on, but that first night of each week was hard because I wasn't able to sleep much before going to work.

When new positions became available within the company, they were posted in the break room along with a list of the requirements and responsibilities. Bidding on a job was fairly easy. There was a sign-up sheet attached to the bottom of each posting. If you were interested, you just signed your name to the sheet. There was a date when each bid would close. Once the bid closed, the warehouse coordinator would sit down and figure up the points of each person who placed a bid. Points were based on attendance, any disciplinary action you may have received, and your time of service with the company. Whoever had the most points had the job, unless it was a position that required previous experience.

In April 1994, I signed a bid to be a forklift driver

in the same department. I figured this had to be easier than selecting. About a week after signing the bid, I found out that I had gotten the job. I was looking forward to the change but was a little nervous also. I had driven a forklift a little, but not the kind you stand up on. The only one I had messed with was one that you sit down on, and it ran off gas or diesel. The forklifts at Food Lion were weird looking and electric. I hadn't seen any like this where I came from.

Eventually my first day came and it was ugly. I didn't tear anything up, but I needed a football field of room to keep from running over someone. When I was moving, it was running very slow. I had to twist my head around because I didn't know enough to turn around backwards and drive the lift as the more experienced people did. The warehouse had a railroad spur line in the middle of it, and I was a nervous wreck driving down by it. However, after a few weeks I got the hang of it and, after a couple months, I could turn around and drive as well as the more experienced operators could.

I was assigned to the freezer where the temperature was anywhere from ten above to ten below zero all the time. It was cold and what was even worse, I had to do more riding from aisle to aisle in my new job, than I did walking and lifting in my old job. While selecting, you could walk the entire freezer from start to finish, and the exercise kept you somewhat warm. Forklift drivers were allowed to come out of the freezer for ten minutes every hour, which helped. Anyway, I got the hang of it and eventually got to where I could do pretty well with the job. I could put the lift anywhere I needed it, figured out what to wear to stay warm, and learned how to run each aisle so that I stayed ahead of the selectors.

I continued to drive the forklift for six months until a job came open in the transportation department. The position title was a fuel jockey. The job consisted of fueling each tractor trailer that came in off the road, adding oil or water when needed, and making sure the trucks were clean. I felt this was just where I needed to go so that I could get my foot in the door to drive. However, I had no idea of all that would happen before I'd get there.

To begin with, the other associates gave me a hard time. They couldn't understand why I would leave my job for one that paid three dollars less an hour. What they didn't know was that I lived at home with Mom and Dad. I had paid off my truck by this time, and I had no other bills to pay except for car insurance each year. The rest of my paycheck was mine to keep. Taking a pay cut was not going to hurt me that much, and I figured it would pay off in the long run if I could get the driving job I wanted. Nevertheless, they laughed at me and told me how stupid I was, but I knew my day would come.

The other problem I had was from my manager and his staff. About the same time I signed the bid for the fueling position, we had gotten low on staff in our department. When this happened, management would have everyone work six days a week so that the new hires could work a few less hours a night and get into the swing of things at a slower pace. This made a lot of sense to me, and I was in full support. However, this particular time, they allowed the selectors to work six days, but had the lift drivers working only five days. This made it tough because lift drivers had to stay in front of the selectors to make sure all the slots were kept full. Don't get me wrong, it could be done with some hard work and creativity, but it was tough. So was I.

As we started the six-day weeks, I'd come in every night knowing I was going to have to step it up to stay ahead. We'd start an hour to an hour and a half ahead of the selectors so we would have time to set up our aisle. Each night I was able to keep up, but many nights I couldn't come out of the freezer for the first two, or sometimes three, hours, otherwise I'd get behind. It wasn't only me getting behind, but all the forklift drivers would get behind if they came out. The company said we could take a break to get warm, but I just wanted to be able to keep up with all the extra people. However, this was short lived.

One night I stayed in the freezer from 7:30 p.m. until 11:00 p.m., which is when break time was called. I was fairing pretty well except for my feet, which were freezing. I went outside and sat for fifteen minutes and when break was over, I went into the break room on the way back to my lift and got a candy bar. The lead person over the forklift drivers was in there. He told me I needed to get back down on my aisle. I told him I would as soon as I went to the warmup room to let my toes thaw out because I had been down there for over three hours. He looked at me and told me that I needed to get my ass back down there now. I quickly got angry and told him if he wanted that forklift on that aisle that bad, the keys were in it (I will leave the ugly words I used out of this), and that I was going to get warm before I went back. After all the stepping up, I had done, and this was how I was going to be treated. I was mad!

At about 4:30 a.m., I was getting ready to go home when I was called into the office. When I walked in, I noticed that all the lead people were there. There were five people including the lead lift driver I'd had words with earlier. My manager asked me why I spoke to the lead man the way I did earlier in the breakroom, and I told him because he talked to me that way first. The manager asked me why I wasn't taking my warmup time like I should have each hour, and I informed him that it was impossible because of the number of selectors we had working. We just couldn't keep up if we came out every hour for ten minutes. The manager told me that I did not need to talk to the lead man the way I had. He told me my production was fifteen drops an hour, and I needed to take my warmup time when it was scheduled. I told them if that is what they wanted, then that is what they would get. Little did I know what would happen next.

The next night I came in and got my drops. I counted two hundred drops. This was one hundred more drops than on a big night. This was huge! A lead man who was in the office the morning before was standing next to me and I told him how many drops I had and that I would need some help. He blew me off. So, I just went on about my business and began my night as I always did. The only thing I did differently was that when my fifteen drops had been made each hour, I would come out of the freezer for ten minutes. I did this, just as I was instructed, all night.

On my way to lunch, I went by the shipping office. When I walked to the window, I noticed that selectors had hung the entire window frame with labels, all the label boards were full, and there was a man in the back cutting out cardboard to make more room for more labels. A label was what the selectors placed on each box they selected. If they got to a slot where there was no product, they would hang the label on the windowsill and it was up to the lift driver to get it. All the labels in the office were mine, but I didn't let it bother me. I went on to lunch. After all, my fifteen drops were done for that hour, and it was time to eat and get warm. I was not going to disobey my manager.

When lunch was over, I was down working on my section. I looked up, and coming down the aisle toward me were the manager, his boss, and every member of management for that department. It looked like a posse in a western movie. Everyone who was in the office the morning before was lined up behind the manager. The manager walked up to the lift, twisted his neck, and asked me what the problem was. I smiled real big and proudly said, "There is no problem. In fact, I want to shake your hand, because up until tonight I had been staying in here trying to do a good job, going above and beyond my job description, so I could stay caught up and we could get out of here. However, after our talk yesterday morning, I haven't gotten anywhere near as cold, and I'm not half as tired as I have been in the past. Thank you for setting me straight."

Man, you talk about pissing someone off! I had done it. He twisted that necktie around, his face turned red, the other supervisors kind of snickered, and they all walked off. Everything I had tried to tell him would happen, had. And by doing my job just like he'd instructed me, there was nothing he could say to me. He had made a fool out of himself in front of his boss and his managers. Even though I didn't like this manager, I still learned a couple of things from him. First, I learned that if I ever got into management, this wasn't how you treat people. I think God gave us two ears and one mouth so we can listen twice as much as we talk. I felt that if the manager had listened to me instead of just spouting out rules, this situation could have been avoided. Second, I learned that you can't make assumptions about a person based on their appearance. This manager assumed that because I talked a little slower that I was not that smart. I, on the other hand, assumed that, because he was a manager, he would act in a way that was best for the company and the employees. Boy, were we both wrong! I learned that he didn't have a clue about how to handle business. His assumption about me resulted in his being embarrassed in front of his boss and peers.

A few days later, the manager pulled me to the side and asked me why I signed up for the fueling position. I told him because I wanted to drive a truck for the company sometime in the future and wanted to get my foot in the door. He told me that if he had anything to say about it, I would never drive a truck for Food Lion. I told him I still wanted to go. He told me that I was stupid for wanting to take a cut in pay, and that the transportation supervisor would want to talk to me. He said the transportation supervisor would ask me about the episode a night or two earlier and about some damage I had done to a wall a year earlier with the pallet jack (which was not my fault). I told him I still wanted to go.

The following night, my manager told me that he and I were going to meet with the transportation supervisor about 4:00 a.m. When the hour came around, we walked up to the front of the warehouse into a closed office. The transportation supervisor was a big, tall guy, with some grayish hair, and very well dressed. After talking to him for just a few minutes, I could tell he was down to earth. His name was Don Ellis. We sat down and Mr. Ellis explained to me what the fuel jockey job consisted of. He asked me if I could drive a truck and I told him I could. He asked what kind of experience I had. I told him that I'd been driving with dad and my uncles for years. I also told him I had my class B CDL, which I hadn't had for long, but I was still proud of. He said, "Well, if you want the job, be there Monday evening at 3:00 p.m. to start." Then he ended the conversation. He never asked me anything else. My manager never said anything, but I think it upset him a little that the transportation supervisor didn't ask me anything that he wanted him to. I was just happy I wouldn't have to work with him anymore, and by going to the fuel island, I was getting closer to my dreams.

4

Fuel Island

This chapter and the next, although short, are an important part of my career. For someone who wants to move up in their career, I would suggest they keep in mind that every position is a stepping-stone toward their goal.

I started on the fuel island in September 1994. I was the last of a four-man team. Our schedule had us starting each day at 3:00 p.m. and working until about 11:30 p.m. Each of us had about 20 trucks a night to fuel and wash, except on Wednesday and Thursday when we had about 27 because of trucks that came in on our days off. We would start the week on Monday, washing every truck on our line. We cleaned the cab, wheels, fuel tanks, and mud flaps. We did this every Monday unless it rained, which would put us washing on Tuesday. Our goal was to wash everything we could at the beginning of the week, so we could coast through the rest of the week.

The crew on the fuel island were noticeably neat and organized. Each day we'd all arrive and clock in at the same time. We all had our own wash buckets that were kept locked up in our back room. We'd get them out, along with our five-gallon buckets of Purple Stuff and head to the wash pit. Before any truck was brought over, the wash pit had to be set up. Five hoses that were on poles were pulled out so that there was a hose on each side of the four trucks we were washing. Then we filled up our wash buckets with soap and water to sit in front of each truck. The buckets had wheels on them so we could roll them from one side of the truck to the other if we needed to. The last thing we did was place a five-gallon bucket of Purple Stuff on each side of the four spaces. This allowed us quick access to the truck cleaning chemical while we worked on the wheels and tanks of the tractors.

Once all of this was done, we would walk to the truck line and get any truck off our assigned line that was backed into a parking space. Anytime a truck had been used, the driver would back it into a parking space to let us know it was ready for cleaning and fueling. After fueling the truck, we added any necessary fluids the driver had requested, then we washed it. We would then park the truck back on the line by pulling it nose first into the parking spot. When we got out of the truck we were finished with, we'd lock the door and get another one off the line. We repeated this routine the entire night.

The job was very easy as long as you used your time wisely and completed your work. If it rained, we didn't wash, only fueled. If a thunderstorm came up, then we went into our little office and sat until it passed, no matter how long it took. The job may have paid less, but it was much easier, and I knew I was getting my foot in the door to eventually drive. However, being only nineteen years old meant I would not qualify to drive a truck with this company until I turned twenty-one. In addition, although I'd been learning to drive for a long time, I did not have any verifiable experience. I spoke to my supervisor about this, and he suggested I go to truck driving school. It was cheap, short term, and counted as a year of experience. I spoke to some of the drivers and found that some of them had done the same thing.

I started truck-driving school in June of 1995. It was

a sixteen-week class that consisted of practicing maneuvering a tractor-trailer around an obstacle course, city driving, and written assignments. I had a good time at school. I had been around trucks all my life, so it was like a walk in the park for me on most things. The hardest thing to learn was getting the trailer around, because I had driven more straight trucks than tractor-trailers. The class was from 11:00 a.m. to 4:00 p.m. five days a week. My supervisor told me I could come in at 5:00 p.m. instead of 3:00 p.m. until I finished school, which put me working until about 1:30 a.m. to get my work done.

The schedule wasn't too bad. I would get in the bed every night about 2:30 a.m. and get up around 8:00 a.m. to be at school by 10:00 a.m. (I've always thought it good practice to plan to arrive early to appointments if possible. This way if you have a problem along the way, you may be able to resolve the issue and still be on time.) I was getting decent rest every night, and I was having fun. Taking this course also enabled me to have my class A CDL before I turned 21.

Once school was over, I got an opportunity to drive a truck during the day for one of my dad's friends, Larry Barbour, and eventually for my dad. I did it just to help them out and to gain some experience that I needed in order to get to where I wanted to be. This would prove to be a little tough though, as I was starting about 7:00 a.m. for Larry, working until 4:30 p.m., and then going to work at Food Lion until about 2:00 a.m. Sleep was not a problem when I got a chance to rest, so I stuck with it. I was determined to get the experience I needed to get the job I wanted. Besides, I could not ask for a better teacher. My dad knew how to drive a truck without destroying it, and he wanted me to learn how to drive the right way. I'm sure he would have rather I'd gone to college, but if I was going to drive a truck, he wanted me to know how to do it the right way. Many drivers, especially in today's world, do not have that kind of opportunity. Little did I know, this was the start of something much more than just driving a truck. My life was taking a turn. I was so busy juggling learning to drive with my night job, I did not even realize it.

Don Ellis, our supervisor on the fuel island, was good to us. There was one thing he did during my time at the fuel island that I will never forget. One Sunday he asked all four of us if we would come in to wash trailers out on a Sunday while they were all sitting still. He told us we'd be paid overtime and we'd be done around 3:00 p.m. When we got there that morning, he got us all set up on where we would be working. I was on the backside of the warehouse. They had the trailers lined up in a row. I went from trailer to trailer washing with a pressure washer. I didn't know what he had the other guys doing because they were on the other side of the building.

Later that day, he came around to check on me and I noticed he was as dirty as I was. After talking to him a little bit, I found out that he, too, had been washing trailers. Imagine that! A supervisor working beside the lowest people on his payroll. I couldn't believe it. In the year and a half that I'd worked in the warehouse, I had never seen a supervisor get out and do any kind of manual labor. To have someone of Don's standing work beside us, showing he wasn't above doing the same dirty job we had to do, amazed me.

From that moment on, I had the utmost respect for Don Ellis. He had the same passion and way of thinking that my family had during my childhood. He wasn't scared to roll up his sleeves and get his hands dirty, which is something that many people forget when they get into management. Little did I know, his influence would play a much bigger part in my life as my career progressed beyond my expectations.

5

Switcher

May 24, 1997, I married Julie Smith and we resided in Erwin, NC. I worried about our finances, as my fuel island job didn't pay that much, and we had purchased our first home instead of renting. In October of 1997, a switcher position came open on the yard, which paid more. Switchers were employees who moved the trailers around on the yard to have them loaded or unloaded. They drove little single axle trucks with no suspension, a fifth wheel that moved up and down by hydraulics, and a sliding rear door for easy access to the air lines and electrical cord. I thought a switcher position might be a good opportunity for me to gain some more experience toward moving into a driving position.

I put in for the job and started near the middle of October. It was a hard job at times and easy at other times. There were times when it seemed like everyone in the warehouse wanted a trailer moved all at the same time. Then other times no one wanted anything moved, so we sat around and talked.

One of my colleagues, Ray Hobbs, from the fuel island had gotten on as a switcher just a couple months before me. He and I ended up working together. He was great to work with. He didn't complain, he worked hard, and he knew what he was doing. Within a couple weeks after I started, we knew what each other was doing all the time. We knew how to make each move count so that we didn't waste time riding around the warehouse without a trailer.

Our schedules were not so bad either. One week we would work four nights of second shift and on Friday we would come in around 5:00 p.m. and work until 5:00 a.m. Then we would have Saturday and Sunday off. To me, this was the hardest week, because it took me away from home five nights in a row. On top of that, I was still working during the day getting some local driving experience, so sleep was a precious commodity.

Then the next week we would work second shift Monday and Tuesday night, then be off on Wednesday, and work first shift on Thursday. On these weeks, we would work second shift Friday and day shift on Saturday. I liked this schedule because it allowed me to be at home two more nights a week. Each week, the person working Monday through Friday was by himself on the yard on Wednesday and Thursday night, which was the hardest of all. Everyone in the entire warehouse had to depend on one switcher to move every trailer in the yard. Many of these nights, you wouldn't even have time for a break. The plus side of it was that the warehouse usually finished up a little early, so you'd have time at the end of your shift to take a breather and finish the rest of your moves. I knew that the schedule was sometimes tough to meet, but the other switchers and I liked the time we had at home, so we just took the good with the bad and carried on.

Near the end of my time as a switcher, I accidentally smashed my finger in the sliding door of the switcher truck and ended up needing stitches. I remember going to the fuel island and sitting down because I was almost ready to pass out. Don Ellis was still the transportation supervisor and someone went to get him. He came over and asked me if I was all right. I showed him my finger and told him I would be fine. He told me I might need stitches and had the lead driver take me to the hospital. Stitches wouldn't be enough to hold me back from reaching my goal, though. After I was done getting stitched up at the emergency room, I went back to work. This job was not going to whoop me.

Soon after my emergency room visit, Don had our lead driver, Ronnie Williamson, give me a road test. Finally, the moment I had been waiting for had arrived! I knew I could do it, but I was still nervous. I had been in a truck with many different people, but this is the one time in my life that I had to be as impressive as I could be. Here I was a twenty-three-year-old young man, still wet behind the ears, interviewing for a job that many veteran drivers would love to have. This was no longer training. This was sink or swim time.

Ronnie asked me if I could come in early one morning for the test and of course, I said yes. I had told my dad that I was getting a shot at a road test and he was happy for me. He began testing me by asking questions they might ask. He wanted to be sure I remembered everything I had been taught. I was glad he did, because I had to be able to show my stuff when the time counted.

The morning I got there, we went and got a truck off the line. We then found a fifty-three-foot trailer to hook up to. Once the hook-up was complete, I began doing my pre-trip inspection. I went over everything I could see, touch, or even imagine on the truck, which took almost thirty minutes. I remember thinking, "I hope he doesn't deduct points from me for taking so long." I just kept on, thinking it would be better to take a little longer and show I knew the parts of a truck, than it would be to skip a bunch of stuff and look like some other 'steering wheel holders.' That's the term used for someone who considers him- or herself to be a truck driver but doesn't really know what they're doing.

Once the pre-trip was done, we got in the truck and started down the highway. He told me not to be nervous, to take my time, and do the best I could do. We went up highway 301 into Dunn, NC. This highway made a left and then a hard right turn, which I knew and had dreaded. I'd played this in my mind so many times as to how I was going to handle this, and I hoped a car was sitting in the way when I got there. As nervous as I was, I needed the obstacle to prove I could handle the job. As I approached this intersection, the light was green, but once I got up to it, the light turned red, which meant I had to stop. This was good because it allowed traffic to my right the possibility to thin out before I made my right turn.

Well, just my luck, traffic did thin out, but in the time it took their light to turn red and mine to turn green, there were a few cars sitting there in my way, which was good for me. I proceeded to pull out and swing as I normally would, which I knew would cause traffic to have to back up. I pulled across the intersection, placed the nose of the tractor close to the front of the first car, and stopped. One by one the cars began to back up and eventually I had enough room to make the turn and keep the trailer off the curb. I was so proud of myself for doing this, and Ronnie even complimented the way I had handled the obstacle. This was the positive reinforcement that I needed to complete the test.

We continued up highway 301 until we got into Benson, NC. Ronnie asked me to make a right turn and go down Main Street. This was a hard turn also because you didn't have much room, plenty of traffic to deal with, and a light pole on the corner of the street that I had to miss with the trailer. I proceeded with this obstacle just as I had done with the last one. Next thing I knew we were headed down main street in

Benson. This was the second of the three hardest parts of the test, and I had done it beautifully.

We went to the end of town and got onto Interstate 95 to go back to the warehouse. Ronnie began asking me how long I had been driving and I told him for about eleven or twelve years. He asked who my teachers had been. I explained to him about my dad and uncles teaching me so much and told him I had also been to school. He didn't say a whole lot, just that he thought I was doing a good job. This meant a lot to me. If I could only be just as impressive in the backing exercise that I had to do next.

Upon returning to the warehouse, Ronnie asked me to stop and let him out. He told me to back into an open door and he would watch me. I pulled out into the parking lot, as nervous as I could be, and proceeded to back the seventy-foot, hinged in the middle unit to the dock. And, what do you know? I bumped it perfectly the first time! I was so proud of myself for what I'd done. I recall thinking of my dad and uncles and how much they had helped me get to this point.

Once the backing exercise was over, we parked the truck and went inside the transportation supervisor's office for the moment of truth. Ronnie told Don that I had done an outstanding job and that my shifting was better than most veteran drivers. Don told me that was good and asked me to come see him in a couple of days.

When I returned to see him, Don closed the door and told me he would have to write me up for smashing my finger in the door of the switcher. My heart sank. I felt like the driving job I had been longing for was slipping away from me. I told him that I didn't feel that was fair because almost everyone in this world has smashed their finger in the door of a car or truck sometime in their life. His response was, "Don't worry about it. I am putting you on the road."

I was as relieved as any one person could get. All the hard work and dedication that I had put in for five years was finally going to pay off. I remember Don handing me the constructive advice memo for smashing my finger in the door to sign. I handed the signed paper back to him and he began handing me other papers to fill out for my new driving job. I had to be the only person in history to be written up and promoted on the same day at the same meeting.

As proud as I was, I began to think about all the people who had helped me get the position. There was, of course, my entire family of truck drivers, and two mechanics in the truck shop, Termite and Lawrence, who I had always looked up to. I even thought of those 'steering wheel holders' that considered themselves truck drivers but tore up a lot of stuff making for costly repairs. I had learned as much from them as I had from the professionals. Because of them I knew what not to do. I also remember thinking very highly of Don, the transportation supervisor, and the lead driver. These two gentlemen had given a twenty-three-year-old kid a chance at a job that many older drivers would have loved to have. They trusted that I could handle the job and for that, I was so appreciative. I would also learn down the road that this still was not the end of Don Ellis's positive influence on me, which gets even more amazing as the years pass.

6

Driving and Making Friends

I started driving on May 5, 1998. This was a Monday, and I would have to stay with a trainer through Saturday, with Wednesday off. My trainer had been with the company for much longer than I had been, and he had been driving the entire time. On our first day out, we went to Wilmington, NC to unload and then on to Conway, SC to pick up a load of charcoal to bring back to the warehouse. I remember thinking on that first day how easy the job was compared to the trucking I was used to. When we got to the store, the only thing we had to do was help push the product, which had already been palletized, off the truck. How much easier and simpler could life get?

This was all we did the first week. The trainer did most of the driving the first day, and the rest of the week we took turns. On Friday, he told me I'd be driving all day on my own. He said he wanted to take a nap, which he never did, but it made me feel good that he trusted me so much. When we returned on Friday, he said he was going to let me go on my own on Saturday. This meant a lot to me. Not only was I the youngest driver that Food Lion had probably ever hired, but I was also good enough to go on my own a day early. I was astonished, a little nervous, but I knew I could handle it.

I continued to help my dad during the day for a

while, but eventually had to let that go. I was still dealing well with the hours but had a couple other motorists create some close calls for me. I decided it would be in the best interest of safety for me to focus on one job for a change. However, this didn't last long either.

The trainer had trained a guy named Jeff Emery a month before me. Hillbilly was his handle, and he was hired off the street, so I knew nothing about him. Within a month or so after my training was complete, I got to know Hillbilly. We were on the same shift, which allowed us to run up and down the road a lot together. Hillbilly and I became like brothers in a short period. We came to work each day at the same time, around 3:00 p.m., ran together almost every night, and then we'd hang out at home or run around town together every morning. Many nights we didn't get in until after midnight, and we'd be running around town, loafing, or doing something together by 7:00 a.m.

As Hillbilly and I traveled around delivering product for Food Lion, we were always talking on the CB about something. Most of the time it was nothing important, but it helped to pass the time. One topic we liked to talk about was where we were from. One of my favorite topics was about riding four wheelers in the mountains of West Virginia. The more we talked the more I would tell Hillbilly and the more he would ask. After a couple months of this, he asked me to go look at two four wheelers with him, so I did. We looked at a Polaris Sport 400 and a Honda 250 racer. The 400 Sport was not hurt at all, but the Honda had some blemishes. However, for the price, it still was not a bad deal.

Next thing I knew, I was hauling them home for him and this is when my life took off in the passing lane and never looked back. It was no time before we were headed to West Virginia to ride four wheelers. The first trip was just Hillbilly and me. Of course, my family was there to ride with us, which was good because I was not 100% sure of where I was going on the trails.

Riding four wheelers in the mountains became a big thing. In fact, it became much bigger than I could have ever imagined it would. Not long after Hillbilly and I became friends, we met another driver named Jeff Jackson who was called Barbeque Kid. Before long, we were all heading to the mountains to ride four wheelers. It went from me and Hillbilly spending so much time together, to all three of us running around together all the time. It was day, night, weekends, holidays, it didn't matter to us as long as we were having fun.

Not long after Kid started hanging with us, we picked up James Autry, who was one of the switchers on the yard where we worked. Then we picked up Paul Griffin who they called Termite, Michael Stevenson who they called Wildman, and Rob Mosher who they called Straight Foot. Then Aaron and Brian Jackson, who are cousins of Barbeque Kid, joined us. We would go about once a month and we'd take our families with us as well as other friends we each had. Things were moving fast, but there was something else going on under the surface that I did not see.

We all became like brothers very quickly. Our families were bonding together, we were constantly on the phone with one another, we knew where each one was all the time, and we helped one another every time we got a chance. It wasn't until 2002 that I realized what else had happened. Some of my family-aunts, uncles, cousins-live in southern West Virginia where we would go to ride our four wheelers. My family members would ride with us and make a point to spend time with us when we came in each month. My family treated every person who visited with the utmost respect. However, it took me a while to realize that I was the link between the two groups of people. When we first started riding together, it was just friends going to the mountains to have a good time as far as I was concerned. I didn't consider myself a leader or anything like that. I was just being me and appreciated the fact that everyone respected me for just being myself.

In 2002, we decided to start our own private campground. We'd been pitching tents and taking baths under a water hose for four years, which had gotten somewhat old. We wanted to get our own place so we could have our own water, our own campers set up, and more room to do what we wanted. When we started planning this, I realized very quickly that this group looked to me for answers. For some reason, they had developed a trust in me that was unreal. Any question that came up was directed to me. I would take the question, ask everyone in the group their opinion, and then offer a decision or solution based on the feedback I'd received. The others seemed to like this and never questioned any decision I made. It was as if they knew I had everyone's best interest in mind.

This was just mind blowing to me. I had never had anyone look up to me as this group did. I was so caught up in being appreciative of being a part of this group that I was just doing what I thought was the right thing to keep us together. I had family members bragging on my friends and friends bragging on my family. It was like I was a link between two different groups of people who had reached a place in their lives that they were lacking in friendship. And though it seemed that way, I knew it wasn't true, because they all had plenty of friends. These groups just clicked so well together that relationships developed that are still strong today. As I said before, I was never popular or associated with a big group of kids at school. So, sitting back and watching two groups of strangers from somewhat different cultures bond so well that they've become family is huge for me. Even more hard to absorb, is knowing that I was a big part of bringing this 'family' together.

We even came up with a name for ourselves. Taking the 'tar' out of North Carolina Tarheels, and the 'billy' out of West Virginia Hillbilly, we are Tar-Billy Cruisers. We are rarely all together at one time, but I surely enjoy every minute of this group's company when we are. I love spending time with these folks. I love helping them. I love talking to them on the phone. Most of all, I am somewhat indebted to them. They are the exact reason this book has Tar-Billy in the title. It was my friends and family who inspired me not only in writing this book, but in many other areas of my life.

This group had more to do with my getting into management than anyone else. They made me see that I had the ability to bring people together. I'd made a positive difference in each of these people's lives, and to know that was worth more than any amount of money. That feeling is something that cannot be purchased, it cannot be given, and it cannot be replaced. I liked this feeling so much, in fact, that I decided I would like to be working in a position to make a difference in other people's lives. I wanted to be the go-to person when something needed correcting. I wanted to be that person that everyone knew would help you if he could. I wanted to be a person responsible for making a difference and seeing a smile on the faces of those that appreciated it, like this group did.

I don't know where I will end up in my life. I may be the next CEO of a major company, or I may fall flat on my face. No matter what, this group of people will have inspired me to try harder than I ever dreamed I would to make a difference in someone's life. Not only the guys, but also their wives, kids, cousins, grandchildren, and even distant relatives that I haven't even met have had a part in this. I know you're thinking, how in the world can someone you have not met have an influence on you? Well, all these people have had good values instilled in them by their families, which goes a long way. In addition, I've heard stories of how each one was raised and things their families did together. Listening to these stories and seeing those values practiced by each one, gives me a deep appreciation for those who have helped them reach that point.

Before I end this chapter, let me say, "Thank you," to all the Tar-Billy Cruisers. If you are reading this book right now, I hope you are enjoying it. I hope it makes as much of a difference in your lives as you all have made in mine. There are very few people in the world who can come together and stick together as we have. You are all very special and I am very proud to consider each of you a member of my family.

7

Getting Out of a Truck

Well, I didn't think it would ever happen, but it did. I finally managed to begin getting bored driving a truck. I'd started learning to drive nineteen years before, and I'd been driving with Food Lion for about seven and a half years. Up until the truck rodeo (truck driving skills competition) in April of 2005, I had spent every minute that I was in a truck trying to prove myself to everyone else. I know that sounds dumb and probably unlike me, but I did. The only conclusion I could come up with was that everyone must feel like they are good at their job to a degree in order to be happy. I felt I had a little more to live up to than most other drivers, because I had the best truck drivers as teachers, my dad and my uncles. I wanted to make them proud of what they had taught me.

However, there was more to this than just proving myself to others. The fact was, for me, there was no longer any challenge in driving. On top of that, Julie was pregnant with our first child, and I wanted to set a good example for him. I had won the rodeo, drove over a half million safe miles just for Food Lion alone, and actually had a few people brag about me. Having accomplished this, I needed something that was going to challenge me the way driving had up to this point. I felt like I was supposed to be doing more in life than driving a truck. Driving a truck is indeed honorable work, but there was a voice inside me saying, "You can do more."

In October of 2005, a lead driver position became open. A lead driver's job consisted of assisting other supervisors and the manager in leading a department of one hundred and seventy people, which I knew would be challenging. I had put in for this position earlier in the year but was turned down. There'd been another applicant who was more qualified at that time. Now things had changed a lot because the transportation manager had been let go, one supervisor stepped down, one transferred to the warehouse, and the present lead driver had been moved up to transportation supervisor. This meant an entirely new crew was going to be running the department. Morale was at the lowest I had ever seen it because of all the "opportunities" that had been brought about in the department.

The new manager who'd been hired was Rudy Peter. He had a passion for success and the knowledge the position required. He found out that I had been interested in the position earlier in the year and asked me if I was still interested. I told him I was, but that my wife was expecting a baby six months down the road and I was afraid that I couldn't make as much money in the office as I could on the truck. He told me I came very highly recommended by the previous supervisors and set a date for us to meet the following week. Not sure what the previous supervisors saw in me, I greatly appreciated their confidence in me.

While I was waiting on the meeting day to come around, A lot of things ran through my mind. Would I be able to afford a pay cut once the baby was born? Was I ready for a change of this magnitude? Would I be able to make a difference in the department and the lives of all the disgruntled associates? Would it affect my friendship with the Tar-Billys?

Would I like it?

We met about 4:00 p.m. one afternoon in his office at the truck shop. I remember being nervous right before the meeting. I had been interviewed by the other manager and some of the questions were difficult. When I entered, he shook my hand and welcomed me in. We made small talk for a few minutes and then we got down to business. Rudy was much more personable than the previous manager. He asked me about previous experience, computer skills, what all I had done at the warehouse, and about everything else you could think of. Rudy explained to me that management was all about serving others, which was great for me to hear because that is why I was there. But I had never thought of it like this. All this time, I had been doing everything I could for the Tar-Billys and did consider myself as a sort of manager of our group, if only by default. But could helping and serving them be why they considered me the leader? At any rate, Rudy was very detailed, and there is one thing he asked me that I will never forget.

He said, "I understand you and some of the other drivers have a place in the mountains where you go four-wheeling." I said, "Yes sir, we do." He said, "How do you think it will affect your friendship with them by being their boss? Because indirectly you will be, and you may have to make a decision one day that they may not like." My exact words were, "These guys are my best friends. They won't receive special treatment, and if they are as true of friends as I feel like they are, they won't put me into that position. If something happens and they make a mistake, they will know I have to do my job." Rudy's response was, "That is good because it can mess up a friendship. But it tells me you've thought it through."

Rudy then explained the pay difference, which turned out, was not as much as I had thought. We talked for about two hours and then he told me to go think about it for a day or two and call him if I had any other questions. I told him that I thought I would take the job, but I would take his advice and think it over for a day or two more.

I went home that night and talked it over with Julie. She left it up to me and said her normal, "If that's what you want to do, then it's fine with me." I admitted to liking the thought of the challenge, but the pay was still my biggest concern. I had a child on the way, and I wanted to support my family. I had always prided myself on earning my own way and making good financial decisions. I wanted to make sure I was putting myself and my family into a position to move forward financially.

I talked about it with my dad. He was supportive, but very hesitant. He knew I had a good job, and I could tell he was worried about me taking on a new role that might mess that up. My dad had taken on new adventures throughout his career, and some did not work out. I understood his concerns but still felt like I needed to do this. I felt like it was time for me to try making a difference in other people's lives on a business level. I felt like the new manager would be a great person to work for, that he would help me if I needed help, and he'd listen to me if I had an idea.

I saw Rudy a few days later and asked where we were on the lead driver position. He said it was mine if I wanted it, and so I accepted it there on the spot. I explained to him that I had thought it over and felt like it was the right thing to do. He appreciated my thinking it through and told me I could start the following Monday.

8

Lead Driver/Supervisor

My last day of being a full-time truck driver was on a Thursday. When I returned to work on Monday, I would technically be a supervisor in training, which meant I had a lot more responsibility. We had a pig-picking at my dad's the weekend before I started my new role. All weekend long, my friends aggravated me about the job. It was all in fun, and just what I needed, as I was a little nervous about starting on Monday. Their jokes and humor helped to calm my nerves.

Monday morning came and I arrived at work around 8 a.m. My first task was to hang around dispatch for a week to learn what goes on in the office. I was also allowed to plunder through cabinets to make myself familiar with all the supplies and paperwork I would need access to later on. If I ran up on something I wasn't sure about, or was just curious about, that week was the time to ask.

The hardest thing I faced the first week in the office was the drivers. Many drivers came up, congratulated me on getting the position, and wished me well in my new endeavor. That part was great and extremely appreciated. However, others asked me all kinds of questions that I didn't have a clue how to answer. They asked about hours, schedules, truck assignments, routing, and many other details. I felt as though I was supposed to have all the answers, and it was only my first week on the job.

Not only did I not have all the answers, neither did I know, in some cases, who to ask to get an answer. Nevertheless, I'd start with my immediate supervisor, move on to Rudy, and then on to whomever he directed me. I discovered very quickly that most people on the management side of the business were very supportive. I felt better knowing that if I was asked a question, I could find someone who could give me a proper answer.

Another interesting thing I found is the drivers just wanted someone to listen to what they had to say. Don't get me wrong, some questions were asked out of selfishness and not based on what was best for the company or group. But many were legitimate concerns. These guys didn't want me to change the world my first day, but they wanted to be heard. As time went on, I learned how to find information to get these guys answers. However, a really important part of returning an answer was to relay it back to the driver in a constructive way. This was huge and, up to this day, a lot of managers and supervisors still do not see the benefit of doing this. It does not have to be an answer they want to hear, just an answer. If it is important enough to an employee to take the time out of his day to bring a concern to a manager's attention, then it should be important enough to the manager to get that employee a response. This is why, as a manager, understanding you are serving others is so important.

Some managers and supervisors are so busy fighting fires that they tend to neglect their employees' needs. The sad part about this is that, in many cases, the fires they are fighting get started because the supervisors are not as organized as they should be. They don't realize that disorganization leads to chaos and employees don't want to work in a chaotic environment.

46

Other managers and supervisors just think it is beneath them to follow up with an hourly associate. These people have forgotten where they came from. They let the job go to their head and they think being manager or supervisor is all about being boss. The reality is being in any management position is all about serving others, which if you recall is something Rudy taught me in my interview. It is all about taking the initiative to roll up your sleeves and find the answer because by doing that you are taking care of your employees' needs. You always want to play the "I'm the boss" card last, and when you do have to play it, you want to be as respectful as possible. Trust me, playing the "I'm the boss" card is usually not good or fun.

I was lead driver for a little over a year, and I learned a lot about people in general. I learned that management could be a great place to be if you really want to make a positive difference. I also learned you need to be thick-skinned and that not all conversations are pleasant. I learned who to go to if I had a problem or did not understand something. One such person was Jim Ryder, the shop supervisor. He was always helping me to better understand the business. He and I developed a great relationship, and I am so thankful for all the advice he gave me throughout my time in this position and my next. He and I are still friends to this day. Overall, I feel like I made a positive difference, and I feel good about my time spent in that position. As I moved up to the supervisor level in February of 2007, I wanted to continue following my dream of making a difference, but it would become more challenging.

Getting a promotion meant more responsibility. I was put on third shift effective April of 2007 for a new delivery model. We went from having 90 drivers on average coming in between 5:00 a.m. - 5:00 p.m. to having the same amount coming in from 1:00 a.m. – 7:00 a.m. In just over a year, I had gone from being a brand new lead driver to a supervisor managing nights. Some nights another supervisor would come in, but most nights it was just me and a dispatcher or two. What I liked about this shift, is that it allowed me to greet every driver on his or her way out the door.

The first few weeks were somewhat chaotic, but we eventually got the bugs worked out, and things hummed along very well. I got to really know the dispatchers and got to know even more about the drivers. If someone had an issue, they came to me. If something went wrong out in the yard or the shop, the problem came to me. I am not sure how, but somehow God allowed me to think things through and make most of the right decisions. Don't get me wrong, I made a wrong decision here and there. Fortunately, these were minor and very rare.

Everything I had learned as a lead driver and a supervisor I liked. I wanted to grow and move on up to become a manager. I wasn't quite sure how I would do this, but I decided I needed to get an associate degree . . . boy would this turn out to be an adventure!

9

Going to College

After being a lead driver for a little over a year and being a supervisor for about three months, I decided I wanted to go back to school. As a 32-year-old father of a one-year-old, this decision would prove to be the biggest and hardest step I would take thus far in my life. I knew that school would be hard and time consuming at best, but I totally underestimated the reality I was in for.

I started at Johnston Community College in Smithfield, NC. The first few weeks were fun and exciting. I met many new people, made some friends, and got in touch with being a kid again. It was neat to sit in a classroom after fifteen years and see how things had changed. I was amazed to see how much more teenagers knew by the time they reached college than when I was in school. This was especially true on current events. It seemed like no matter what the instructors asked, these kids knew something about it. They knew a lot more than I did because I spent most of my time working and what little spare time I had, having fun. Watching the news and learning more about what was going on in the country were just not at the top of my priority list.

After two semesters, I decided to go ahead and get my bachelor's degree, so I transferred to Campbell University in Buies Creek, NC. I wanted to pursue my bachelor's in business administration. This was a step up from an associate degree and came along with a couple more years of school, but I thought it would be best. However, right before I finished my bachelor's degree, I decided to get my master's which added on another year of school.

For three and a half years while at Campbell University, I went to school in the evening, worked at night, and slept usually about four hours per day. Sometimes if I had a test, I would sleep only one or two hours so I could study some more before the test. Almost every Saturday morning I would be at the library on the main campus around 5:00 a.m. I went there early so often that the cleaning people knew me and would speak to me when I walked in. I usually stayed until around five or six in the evening or, if I had to work, until around two in the afternoon. Sunday was a repeat of Saturday. I got so tired of studying I didn't know who I was. On top of the time I put in, I had to pay for it. I made too much money to get any help from the government. However, I did get a discount because my wife worked at the school. Still, it seemed like every time I turned around, the school was asking for two or three thousand dollars. By the time it was all said and done, tuition and books cost me about $50,000.

Finally, after four and a half years since starting at community college, I finished my degrees. I thought I had worked hard to pay for that pickup truck when I was younger! But never have I ever worked as hard as I did for my degrees! I've done many things in my life that I am proud of, but I think these degrees make me prouder than any of my other accomplishments. However, on that same note, it breaks my heart to see other people give up so easily. I know many people who really want to go back to school and who would benefit from it, but they come up with all kinds of excuses as to why they cannot go back. Some say it isn't fair because promotions shouldn't be given based on degrees, but on performance. Unbelievably, I actually agree with that to some extent. Going to college doesn't make you any smarter than the next person. It does broaden your horizons and can help you in so many ways. However, it is still just a process to go through. Once you complete the process, it is up to you to apply your education and your common sense to move forward.

I have heard people say that common sense will get you further than a college education, which I agree with. I know many people without college degrees who have done very well for themselves. Having degrees, however, can certainly open doors for you, but it takes common sense to know which doors to walk through. The bottom line is nothing is impossible if you put your mind to it, but no one can decide your goals except you. Once you make a decision, commit to it. Don't let life, sleep, other people, or even the weather stand in the way of reaching your goal.

10

Challenges at College

During my college career I faced a range of challenges from trying to find a balance of work and school to trying to get enough rest so I could think clearly. The hours were brutal, as there were many twenty- and thirty-hour days. There were even a couple of times when I went forty-eight hours without sleep. I know that may sound a little far-fetched. But there were a few times when I had exams in classes I struggled in. There was no way I was going to let sleep get in the way of passing a class that I had paid to take. As tough as the hours were, lack of sleep wasn't the biggest challenge I faced. What I considered my three biggest challenges were worries over my relationships with my extended family and friends (Tar-Billys), changes in my home life, and depression.

After a while, I began to realize how busy I had become. My family and I used to talk once a week, and now we talked once a month. The only person I talked to on a regular basis was my dad. He worked mornings and I could call him on my way to school. Communicating with my friends was not much better. I went from talking to them once every week or two to once every couple of months. This decrease in communication led me to start worrying. I wondered if my friends and family would think I was ignoring them. Would they understand why I didn't call and how busy I was? Would they think what I was trying to do was stupid? However, I started paying closer attention to our interactions, and I noticed that anytime I was around them they always treated me just like old times. If I called them, we would talk as if we had just hung up from one another. They laughed and joked with me as if nothing was different. If something was going on and I said I had to study, they didn't beat me up about it or discourage me. In fact, they seemed to support me and that was a great feeling to have. Noticing these things, my worries subsided. Instead of calling my dad every day, I began calling other family members or friends so that I could stay in touch with everyone.

A man once told me that most people could count their true friends, the ones they could really depend on, on one hand and have fingers left over. Going back to school proved that I was fortunate enough to have more friends than I could keep up with, which was one of the best feelings in the world. My Uncle Randy would say, "I don't know how you pick your friends, but whatever you're doing, you're doing a good job at it." That statement alone made me feel good, but little did he know, I used the same methods he and the rest of my family did. I learned what I knew through them.

The more I thought of my friends and family, I realized I was not the only one making sacrifices in going back to school. My friends and family were, too. I decided I wanted to do something to tell the world about all these people and the inspiration I have drawn from them, but I struggled with how to do that. I thought about television, but my name is not big enough to even get in the restroom at a television studio, much less in front of a camera. I thought about radio, but the signal only broadcasts so far and I wanted the whole world to hear what I had to say. All I knew was I wanted to let the world know how proud I was of these people, and I didn't have a clue how I was going to do it. Even though I had to step away from them for a while to accomplish what I have accomplished, they are a huge inspiration behind what I have done.

During my time as a supervisor, I was required to write an article for our department newsletter once a month. When I first started writing, I would write about things going on within the department, like safety, load conditions, or truck driving in general. Then one day, I decided to write something different. I wrote an article about getting to know the associate sitting next to you. Now this article got some laughs and some raised eyebrows, but at least people read it. However, I figured they wouldn't read anything else I wrote after that. Boy, was I wrong.

I enjoyed writing the article on getting to know your fellow associate, so I ventured into other areas involving life. I began having people come tell me how they liked my articles, which made me feel good. Eventually I wrote one on negativity that a few associates didn't like. In fact, some complained to my manager. My boss informed me of what had been said, but he never told me to stop writing. I almost did anyway. When I first heard the complaints, my initial thought was that I better back off before I get into trouble. However, after some more thought on the matter, I recalled something a very famous racecar driver said once. "It doesn't matter if the people in the stands cheer me or boo me when I am introduced or get out of a car at the end of a race, as long as they do something is what counts." The name of this driver is none other than the late great Dale Earnhardt.

It dawned on me that even though some people didn't like what I had written, they continued to read my articles. Therefore, my writing was interesting enough to keep them coming back for more. I was going to keep writing newsletter articles because I enjoyed it so much and many of my readers seemed to enjoy it. Writing the articles also helped me gain practice in writing and in knowing what people like to read. All of this put together helped me decide the best way to announce to the world how proud I am of my friends and family. That is how the idea of this book came about.

At JCC, I was going to school in the morning until around noon. When I transfered to Campbell University, classes were in the evenings. This made my home life much harder than I had been accustomed to while at JCC. It got to where I would go a week at a time without even seeing my wife or son. I was rarely home, and when I was there, I was asleep or doing homework. I didn't have time to go do anything as a family. Due to working nights, my schedule stayed so messed up that I never felt good when I was at home, and I was always extremely tired. Fortunately, between my wife, her parents, and my parents, they kept up with my son so I could do what I needed to do. There were many family functions on my side of the family that my wife and son attended that I did not. And then there was Cody, my son. When I first started school, he was only a little over a year old. He was walking, trying to talk, and getting to be more fun by the day. As time went on, he began asking questions about where I was going and when I was coming home. He would have my wife call me at night so he could ask me where I was and when I was coming home, and to tell me he loved me. Many nights his phone calls brought tears to my eyes. Between school and work, sometimes I wondered if what I was doing was even worth it. I always came to the same answer. I knew it was.

I knew that if I was going to complete my degree, I needed to do it while Cody was still small. It was my plan to be finished school by the time he was four and a half. By that time, Cody would be at a good age to begin doing things like fishing, hunting, and going into the mountains with me, and

I would be in a place where I could spend a lot more time with him. I also felt that completing my education would set an example for him. On my first day at Johnston Community College, an instructor told all the students that most kids would go to college if their parents went to college. Although I knew this would not ensure my son would go on to college when the time came, I knew it couldn't hurt. I wanted him to know he could go anywhere he wanted in life. Giving up was not the example I wanted to give him.

As I entered my second year of college, I began getting upset for no reason. I could be driving down the road, watching something on TV, or hearing about something sad in the news and become upset. This was especially true when it came to seeing kids being hurt on television. Having a son of my own, I hated to see him or any other child in pain. The first time or two it happened, I blew it off thinking my reaction was just stress, but it got worse. This issue was on the verge of becoming obvious to those around me. In fact, there were times when I had to walk away from conversations to keep anyone from knowing.

One day, before going to sleep, I saw a commercial on TV advertising a new drug on the market to treat depression. The commercial listed some of the symptoms of depression and as I watched, my mind began wondering. Could I be suffering from depression? At first, I thought there was no way I could be suffering from any kind of depression. I, of all people, was supposed to be strong and not let stress affect my emotions. People expected me to be able to handle whatever was thrown at me. Moreover, I expected myself to be able to handle anything that was thrown at me. I did some research on the subject and came to the conclusion that depression could very well be my problem. But why would it be happening to me?

After some reflection, I noticed a pattern in my life. Everywhere I went, day to day, week to week, I was always alone. Since transferring to Campbell and going to school in the evenings, I was home alone during the day. Even though I'd made some friends at school, we weren't close like I was with the Tar-Billys and my family. However, because of school and work I didn't get to see my Tar-Billy friends and family often. I faced a similar situation at work. I had many friends at my job and although I would get to see Termite and Straight Foot many mornings, I still wasn't as close with the others as I was with the Tar-Billys. I did consider Rudy and Jim to be close friends of mine, but they worked first shift, so I rarely saw them. If I went to lunch during the night, I went by myself and ate alone. Virtually everything I did, I did it alone. Don't get me wrong, sometimes it was nice to be alone to clear my head. I had a lot going on between being a daddy, a husband, and a supervisor, plus trying to earn a degree, learn management, and occasionally spend time with my friends. If all those things were not enough, in May of 2008 I started writing this book. But all the time I spent alone made me very isolated.

In discovering that I was quite possibly depressed, it was time to figure out what to do about it. Going to the doctor was out of the question for me, because I expected a doctor would want to write me a prescription. As far as I was concerned, medicine was not an option. With the hours I put in each day/week, I didn't want anything in my body that might impact my ability to stay awake or think clearly. I had to figure out how I was going to juggle everything and keep my sanity on my own.

I can remember author and motivational speaker Lou Tice, someone I have a lot of respect for, stating many times, "If you envision yourself succeeding and focus on that, then you will succeed." With Lou's advice, why couldn't I solve this by myself? All I had to do was focus on what I wanted the final outcomes of my future to be.

I began thinking about getting my degree, spending more time with family and friends once I got out of school, finishing a cabin we had started building, and advancing my career once I received my degrees. I thought of my wife and our goal of eventually getting a bigger house with some acreage. I thought of Cody and about focusing more of my time on watching him grow and change. Anything that was a positive target to achieve in my future, I thought about every chance I had. Like planning my graduation party. I imagined it would be a pig-picking at my dad's. I'd invite all my friends and family to help me celebrate. At a lot of graduation parties people bring gifts, but not this one. No one was to bring a gift or anything. They were just to show up and have fun. There would be some games played and I would DJ the entire event. I would wait for everyone to start eating and I would use the opportunity of having everyone together to announce this book. I hadn't told anyone I was writing it yet, but my graduation party would be the perfect opportunity for me to share this news with all my family and friends as a "thank you" to those who inspired and supported me.

Writing this book is something that helped me the most through my depression. Writing was therapeutic. It became a way for me to focus on the positives in my life. Although focusing on positive thoughts and goals helped, sometimes it was still rough going, because keeping happy thoughts is not as easy as it sounds. Especially when outside stressors are still present. There was always someone wanting more from me, always something requiring my attention, and always something trying to drag me back down. During these times, I tried to keep the perspective that I had put myself in this situation, no one else did. But I had done so in order to benefit my family's future, and I reminded myself that school would be over at some point soon.

I began to set goals to help me get through and to hopefully take some of the stress out of the day-to-day grind. One goal I set was the writing of this book. I had been trying to write only in my spare time, but I had so little spare time. Therefore, I decided to make it part of my day. Each day, I required myself to write 500 words. They didn't have to be words ready for a publisher, and they didn't have to be perfect, but they had to be written. I figured, if I could hold myself to 500 words per day, it wouldn't take up much of my time and the book would be finished by the summer of 2011. Besides, I could only sit in front of the computer long enough to write 500 words before falling asleep. In fact, some days I couldn't type 500 words. When that happened, I would hold myself to 1000 words the next day. Reaching these smaller goals gave me a feeling of accomplishment in my heart. My larger goal was 50,000 words, and once I reached 20,000, I began to feel better and better about hitting my target. It was as if my future was getting clearer and clearer with every letter leading to every word. Putting my thoughts and memories onto paper, and focusing on a tangible goal, helped me to overcome my depression.

11

Dealing with Frustrations

Each of us has a different purpose in our life which sets us apart as the great individuals we are. However, we all hold one thing in common. Most of us must work to make a living. I think we can all agree that every job has its pros and cons, and at times things can be frustrating. No matter the profession, there is something that frustrates us each and every day while trying to get our work done. Do we view frustrations as a chance to grow? Can we learn from frustrations? How do we handle frustrations day in and day out?

Sometimes things are frustrating because we allow them to be. When something doesn't go our way and we get bent out of shape about it, it is frustrating. However, if we look at the situation as an opportunity to make a positive improvement, then we have begun looking at a solution instead of a problem and the frustration begins to diminish. I heard it said once that the most successful people are those who deal with frustrations better than others. I think there is a lot of truth to that statement.

Think back to when you graduated high school. You had the whole world in front of you and not a clue what to do with it. You may have struggled to buy a car, find that right job, save enough to buy a house, and figure out how to pay all the bills that followed. On top of that, as a young adult, you wanted to go off on the weekends to have a good time. But that took money. Wasn't it frustrating to be the one receiving the paycheck but spending it on what seemed like everything but yourself? How did you deal with this? We have all been there, and we all understand how frustrating life can be in general. However, by focusing on solutions we are often able to overcome the frustration and move on.

Frustrations can come in many different forms. If we plan to go to the store, we expect the car to start when we get ready to leave. If it doesn't start, then it can be frustrating. When we get to the store, we expect to find exactly what we are looking for, pay for it, and then go back home. If the store doesn't have what we want or if we are held up in line for a long period of time, then the situation can become frustrating. Whether we realize it or not, for everything we do, we have a mental picture in our mind of how we expect it to work out. When it doesn't work out in the way we've envisioned, we often become frustrated. Our frustration can be over the car starting or a major business decision. I have tried to reduce my own frustrations in life by attempting to view unforeseen situations as challenges, and challenges as opportunities to grow.

Over the last few years, I've put in many hours at work. I've worked 20-hour days and I've calculated as many as 48 hours from the time I woke until the time I was finally able to go back to bed. One of the most frustrating things I've encountered was tolerating these long hours. I am sure you've had days that you knew were going to be long and that you just dreaded getting started. Maybe you had other things you'd rather be doing and getting excited over the long day ahead seemed impossible. Well, I had many such days during the time I was in college. There were times I left home on Sunday night knowing it would be late Monday night or

Tuesday morning before I'd get back home. I'd go to work, then school, then sometimes back to work, sometimes to the library, or just wherever I needed to go to get what I needed done.

My point is that I could have become frustrated and just quit, but I didn't. I was determined to finish school. Finishing school would allow me to advance my career and to make more money to better provide for my family. I wasn't going to let my schoolwork, or my job go lacking because I couldn't get my work done. I was going to make it one way or another. I can remember my parents and my wife telling me that I needed to get some rest. In fact, they would fuss at me sometimes that I was putting in too many hours. I know they had my best interest in mind, and it was appreciated, but I had a goal in my mind that I had to accomplish, and I was not giving up.

Another frustration was not being able to see my family and friends. I'd see my wife and son once or twice a week, but I would be so tired when I was with them that all I wanted to do was sleep. This would frustrate me more than the long days. I wanted to spend time with them, but my body just wouldn't allow it. As a transportation supervisor at the time, I worked nights by myself and was responsible for making sure everything went as scheduled. I was bound and determined not to let the 170 associates under me down. I was going to do my part to make sure those 105 trucks and 350 trailers were where they needed to be. I would see that 264 stores were serviced the way they should be, that my paper was written and turned in on time, that exams were studied for, that classes were not missed. But where and when would I find time to spend with my friends and family?

I wondered about this a lot, especially when I first started school. I'd think back to the question my boss asked me when I first interviewed for a management position. "How do you think your friends working under you will be affected by a decision you may have to make that has a negative effect on them?" My answer was "If they are my true friends, they will trust that the decision I make is right and support me." I'd think back to this conversation often and concluded that this is the way I needed to be thinking. I needed to trust my friends as much as I expected they would trust me. It needed to be a two-way street. Thinking any other way would be selfish on my part or theirs.

The other thing I kept picturing is the final outcome. Much like depression, one key to dealing with frustrations is having a vision of what you want in life and staying focused on the positive. We all had to make sacrifices while I was in school, but I focused on what it would be like to get that degree, to get that better job, or to write a book. I looked forward to spending much more time with my family and friends if I could get all these things accomplished. By getting a degree, I felt it would open a door for my family to have a much better life. I imagined all I could do with a master's degree! I could be the future CEO of a major company, a college instructor, a financial wizard, or anything I wanted to be. Maybe I could earn enough money down the road to make some major improvements on the campground that we were currently having to struggle and save for.

These thoughts kept running through my mind as I went through school. I don't know if this vision was a dream, a goal, a desire, a personal attribute, or whether I was just plain crazy. All I know is I liked the picture enough to keep applying paint, altering it as needed to reflect what I wanted it to look like later on in my life. Many of those long, long days, I didn't even feel like holding the brush. But, I didn't give up. There were frustrations, yes. But by keeping the bigger picture in mind, accepting it as a challenge, and wanting the outcome bad enough, I was able to get through those long days and weeks.

While it helped me with my depression, writing this book has been frustrating, too. As a country boy, I never dreamed I'd be writing a book. I didn't know where to start, and I had no idea how to put it together. I had no knowledge of how to lay it out, or how to get it published. All I knew is I wanted to tell my story. I wanted others to know what they could accomplish, no matter who they are, if they just put their mind to it. Viewing this frustration as a challenge, I worked at writing every time I got a chance, and I researched how to get a book published. Turning this frustration into a personal challenge gave me the opportunity to grow.

12

The Storm

Out of all of the challenges I'd faced so far in my life, none were more difficult than the events of Saturday, April 16, 2011. Having finished my bachelor's, I was working on my master's degree at the time. With finals coming the following week, I needed to study as much as possible. I got up early Saturday, around 5:00 a.m., and headed to the library so I could study before work that evening. I studied until about 2:00 p.m., then went home to eat some before heading to work around 4:00 p.m. Before walking out the door for work, I told my wife I'd be home in 2 or 3 hours. I was just planning on going in to get a few things done before going back to the house to get some sleep. Then I planned to head back to the library early Sunday morning for another day of studying.

The weatherman had been calling for Saturday storms, some of them possibly severe. I didn't pay much attention though, because I'd heard similar predictions in the past, but nothing ever came of them. Not long after I got to work, I got a phone call from an associate at our corporate headquarters informing me there were severe storms in my area. I told him I was aware of the storms and that we were in the process of dropping some refrigerated trailers at some of our stores that had lost power.

About ten minutes after I hung up with him, a tornado warning for our area came across the television in the break room. A minute or two later, one of the drivers, who'd been looking out the door, said he could see it. I walked over to the door and saw the clouds moving faster than normal and debris flying in circles high up in the air. The debris looked like it was moving in our direction, and the wind was picking up.

I told all the associates to get into the bathrooms, and to get away from the windows because I didn't know what else to do. As soon as I spoke, everyone dropped what they were doing and broke into a run. The only female in the office at the time ran into the ladies' restroom. Just before I got to the men's room, the thought hit me that we should stay together in groups of two, at minimum, but at that point there wasn't time to go back. The storm was upon us, and it was fierce. As I waited in the restroom, I tried to find something to get under for further protection in case the roof got torn off. It was the first, and only, time in my life I considered trying to crawl under a urinal. The noise was deafening. The wind roared, breaking glass and slamming doors. I honestly wondered if this was the end for me, but evidently God had another plan.

The storm lasted only about 30 seconds, if that long. Once the tornado passed, we walked out of the restroom and found everything in shambles. The windows were blown out, cracked, or shattered. Debris in the form of ceiling tiles, glass, papers, and anything that wasn't nailed down covered the office. After walking past all the destruction, we exited the building finding even more destruction outside. One side of the warehouse was torn almost completely off. Cars in the parking lot, including mine, were either upside down, on their side, or just destroyed from flying debris. Trailers were turned over, with ammonia leaking from the refrigeration systems. We could hear alarms going off in the distance. It was bad. All I could think of was contacting my family to make sure they were okay.

As I waited for my call to connect, a co-worker mentioned the workers in the warehouse. I immediately hung up before anyone answered the phone and we rushed over. It was the first time in all the Saturdays I'd worked that I realized at that time of day I was the only management person on the entire property. We didn't know who was inside or if anyone was hurt. Since I wasn't familiar with the warehouse part of the facility, I wasn't quite sure how we would account for everyone. When we got to the warehouse, we found a few associates just inside. I asked them to come outside and I started to match up the number of associates with the number of vehicles in the parking lot. (At that time of day, there were very few associates working, so I figured it would be the easiest way to account for everyone, assuming no vehicles had been carried off by the storm.) I found that one of the vehicles in the parking lot belonged to an associate in the computer room who wasn't present. I immediately stopped counting and asked the warehouse workers if they knew how many more people were in the warehouse. The warehouse workers told me that some of their co-workers were on one of the docks just inside the door before the storm hit. I knew we'd need to go inside to find the workers and get them out, but I was concerned about the safety risks as well. I could tell by the way the cold air coming from the freezer was moving that the leaking ammonia was blowing away from us and not toward us. But I was concerned about the stability of the warehouse roof, and we tried to look for any indications it may fall in.

A driver and I quickly ran in and found three workers on the dock. I instructed them to follow us outside. The driver and I went back in, this time to the nearby computer room area, and beat on the door. Fortunately, the associate inside opened the door. She was all right, but scared, like the rest of us. While we were there, the computer room phone rang. It was the same associate from the corporate dispatch office who I'd spoken with earlier. He was checking to see how things were going with the weather. I told him we'd been hit by a tornado. I explained that the warehouse was destroyed, several vehicles were damaged, and I was pretty sure we had an ammonia leak. He instructed me to get everyone away from the warehouse a safe distance away from the ammonia. The three of us went outside, but before moving everyone away from the warehouse, I did another headcount in an attempt to account for everyone. I knew I had accounted for everyone I could, but I also knew it would have been very easy to miss someone. Walking away from that warehouse, wondering whether someone might still be inside either injured or already dead, was tough to do. I didn't care about the warehouse being torn up, the cars and the trailers being destroyed, or any of the material things since they could all be replaced. People's lives however can't be replaced. I knew that getting everyone away from the building and the ammonia leak was the right thing to do. At the same time, walking away from the warehouse without fully checking it for other workers gave me a feeling of giving up on people I worked with and was responsible for. In the meantime, one of the workers had called 911, but was told that first responders would get to us when they could. With so many calls as a result of the tornado, it might be a while.

While we waited, I re-dialed my wife. She was pregnant at the time and I was worried about her and my son. Julie assured me that she was fine and that Cody was at her parents' house. I asked her to call and check on her parents while I called to check on mine. Thankfully, everyone was alright, and I was relieved. That was one worry off my plate, and I could focus solely on the situation at work. Not too much later, some company associates who were trained in dealing with ammonia leaks showed up and searched the facility. Fortunately, no one else was inside, which was another huge relief.

As the evening went on at the warehouse, I found

out through some of my co-workers that some people nearby had been killed in the storm as it moved through the area. One mobile home park just a few miles from the warehouse had been completely wiped out. People lost everything they had, including family members, in less than a minute. As this news soaked in, I had an overwhelming appreciation for life that night. I was so glad to get home around midnight and just put my arms around my family.

I woke early the next morning and went back to the warehouse. I wondered whether I or any of my co-workers would still have a job. I knew I needed to be studying for my exams, but my job was my priority. Without it I couldn't support my family or pay for school. School and exams were the least of my worries that morning.

Upon arriving at work, I spoke to my boss who assured me I still had a job. He explained that the process of moving the business to other locations had already started. He knew I had exams the following week and gave me Monday off to study. I spent the rest of Sunday helping get drivers on the road and assisting with the process of moving the business to other locations.

For the first time in my career, I got to see a contingency plan played out in real life. We moved a huge business in less than 24 hours. It wasn't pretty, but we did it. The storm happened on a Saturday. We started sending drivers out to other warehouse facilities on Sunday to help service our stores from other distribution centers. By Tuesday, all the other facilities had the number of drivers they needed in nearby hotels. On Wednesday, we had to come up with some way of swapping out drivers who had already been sent to other facilities with fresh drivers who hadn't been out at all. Drivers would need to be swapped out once a week. We had about 140 drivers total and 85 had already been sent to other facilities.

I discussed the need to swap out drivers with my boss

and some other colleagues. I suggested we set up a schedule. I knew the drivers had appointments to plan for, kids graduating from high school, weddings, trips, and a laundry list of other prior commitments. I felt that since they were the ones having to be away from home for the next several months while repairs were being made, the least we could do was set up a schedule so they could at least make some sort of plans with their families. Since our office was the only office left standing, what was left of it was swarming with people. You were lucky to get a corner to stand in, much less a desk to sit at. I needed to think, so I told my boss I had an idea for a schedule and asked him to give me about fifteen or twenty minutes to think it through. The only quiet place I could find was the concrete wall outside his office, so I headed that way with a pencil and piece of paper.

I was determined to try to help the displaced drivers and I was not about to let this scheduling business whoop me. I knew how many drivers we had left at our facility, how many had been dispatched to each other facility, and how many each facility predicted they needed on different days. After writing down this information, I sat back, looked at it, and quickly realized it was a play on numbers. All I had to do was use the slower days, when not as many drivers were needed, to swap out drivers. I drew up a rough schedule for each facility and plugged in the numbers. In about fifteen minutes, a base schedule was born, and that same base schedule was used for the next nine months.

A few of the drivers didn't like the schedule, but most were very appreciative. Most drivers understood that the predicament they were in was due to an act of God, and they knew they were fortunate to still have a job. Even though all the drivers weren't happy, it was fulfilling for me to know I had played a part in creating a schedule that made most of the drivers happy. By not giving up and just keeping it simple, I had made a positive difference for the majority. That was why I got into management, to make a positive difference, and I had done that.

The following week, I passed my exams and moved on to new classes. For the next eight months I would go back to supervising night shift and making sure drivers coming and going to other facilities had what they needed. This had its challenges, as I didn't realize how nice it was having all the drivers under one roof until they were scattered out over five different facilities, but each night we worked through each obstacle. The only thing I couldn't continue at that time was writing for this book. There just wasn't enough time for school, work, and writing a book, so I had to put it aside for a while.

13

Graduation

All of my hard work and long days finally paid off. I graduated on December 17, 2011. It turned out almost as I had imagined, but not quite. And though it turned out a little differently, it couldn't have been any better. By the time school was out my body had taken all the abuse it could stand. To celebrate, all I wanted was to have dinner with those closest to me, but my friends and family had something else in mind.

I didn't plan to walk across the stage to get my degree. I was just happy to be done. My final year of school had proven to be even more frustrating than the previous years. I struggled to juggle school, family and friends, and work, especially in the aftermath of the tornado. I was okay with receiving my degree in the mail. But my wife and parents wanted me to walk at my graduation ceremony. So much so, that my parents went to the extreme of arranging with the rest of my family to move the date of our annual family Christmas celebration in West Virginia because it conflicted with my graduation date. Since it was so important to them, I agreed to attend my graduation.

After the graduation ceremony, my wife, kids, parents, and everyone else went back to my parents' house. My uncle and I went loafing around town. We were gone for quite a while and I knew we were supposed to eat dinner at my parents' around 5:00 p.m, so we headed that way. When we arrived, we didn't see anyone outside, but we did see a few cars. I figured everyone was huddled up indoors where it was warm. Anytime our family had get-togethers, we'd hang out in my dad's detached truck shop. My uncle and I headed there. I opened the door to a shop full of people that shouted, "SURPRISE!" There were balloons, a DJ, and all kinds of food to eat. The place was full of family, friends, and even a few people I didn't know. People from near and far had come just to congratulate me. I felt so loved! I cried quite a bit that night, but I assure you they were tears of joy.

Not everyone close to me could make it to the party, which my family and friends had planned behind my back. I seriously had no clue! But with the party being around the holidays, I understood why some couldn't come. One such person was my boss, Rudy. He had made arrangements to go out of town to be with his father for Christmas before the party was planned. However, his wife, Dawn, did come in his place and I thought that was awesome. She's a wonderful lady and I was so thankful she came. Even though Rudy wasn't there in person, I did get the chance to talk to him on the phone. I told him how much I appreciated Dawn coming, and I let him know how much I appreciated him. He was the one person who had inspired me to go back to school and pushed me to do things I thought I never could, which allowed me to build confidence in myself. If it hadn't been for him, I probably never would have gone back. I will always be grateful to him for his inspiration. My life is better now because he chose to believe in me when I did not.

One thing I thought about that night, and still do from time to time, is why all those people chose to spend their time congratulating me that night. I mean, I know they were all there because they liked me, but why did they like me so much? What did I do that was so impressive to make them want to be my friend? It had to be friendship based on personal feelings because I didn't have money, or power, and I've never considered myself to be all that smart.

I treat people the way I want to be treated. I try to be fair and help anyone I can as long as they appreciate it. I work hard, but I like to have fun. I care about others' feelings and try to understand where others are coming from. Regardless, I was still puzzled. Is what I am doing that powerful? Has treating people with respect and dignity become such a thing of the past, that when someone like me comes along, people flock to be next to them? Don't get me wrong, I love my life and everyone in it, but I just don't think I am doing anything that should be considered out of the ordinary.

During my graduation party, my friend Jim Ryder gave a toast on my achievements in front of everyone. During the toast, he made the comment to everyone that he didn't think I realized what I had actually accomplished. To some degree he was right, because I didn't look at what I had done as all that great. I had gone to college and earned two degrees. That was it. Putting in long hours and juggling my workload was certainly a chore, but that is all it was to me. I thought what I had done was something anyone could do if they just set their mind to it.

I guess my point to all of this is, I am just being me. I am not trying to win the affection of others. I do what I do to better myself and because I feel it is right, just like I was taught. I love learning and helping people, I love talking to people, and more than anything, I love to see people smile. I enjoy having people come to me for help knowing I will help them if there is any way possible. My dad once told me that our word is all we really have in life. I believe that he is right.

When we die, some will remember the size of house we lived in or what we were worth. Others will remember the kind of car we drove or the type of vacations we took. However, everyone will remember the value of our word and the kind of person we truly were. This party may have been to celebrate my accomplishments, but those who were there cared for me personally.

It is our word that earns us the friendships we have through our life. If our word is a little shaky, then our friendships will also be a little shaky. If our word has lost its value, then our friendships will quickly lose their value. If our word is good, then we are bound to have good solid friendships throughout our life. Then when times get tough, as they did for me, those friends will be there to support you through the entire process, and in the end, they will celebrate your successes with you. I am here to tell you how amazing it is to have this type of support.

14

Why Do We Do What We Do?

As fast paced as our life can get in this day and time, there are a million things I am inspired to write about. When I was in school a professor asked me a question that got my attention. The professor asked, "Why do we do the things we do?" He was not asking why we work, because we all know the reason we work is to make a living and support our families. He was asking, "Why do we, as human beings, do what we do?" Why do we behave as we do, think the way we do, or just live in general the way we do?

I thought about this a lot and concluded that it boils down to what kind of legacy or memory of ourselves we want to leave behind when we are gone. Think about it for a minute. When we are finally laid to rest, we will be alone in that casket. No one will fill it with money or throw in a friend or family member to keep us company. All that will be left of us is the thought others picture in their mind of us. Do we want people to remember us as a helpful person? Do we want to be remembered for our work ethic, for keeping our word, for treating others fairly, or for our passion to make a difference? We hear statements made all the time regarding someone who passed and how they were fun to be around, how they cared for their family, or how good they were at their job. You could be remembered for any number of different things. But what will stand out the most about you, is how others were affected by you.

That is not to say we should live our lives for others. We live in a country that allows us the freedom to think for ourselves and enjoy life however we would like. Thinking about how one would like to be remembered is different for everyone. Once you decide how you want to be remembered, then your mind will subconsciously guide you to be remembered that way when you die. Those in the military may want to be remembered for their love of their country; a mother, for the way she raised her kids; a firefighter or police officer, for saving people's lives or their service to the community. None of these thoughts are wrong. The one thing that is most important to you, not everyone else, is what matters.

Do we think about this every moment of the day? No, probably not. But it is in our subconscious of everything we do. If you are a person who would like to be remembered for helping others, do you not constantly look for ways to achieve that goal? Our minds are very goal oriented. Once you have made up your mind that you want something bad enough, then your mind normally works toward achieving that specific goal.

A good example of this would be a man I worked with named Emmanuel. I personally never had many dealings with Emmanuel, but the few dealings I had with him were good. Unfortunately, he passed away during his service with our company and I had the privilege of attending his funeral, which was very inspiring. The church was packed to standing room only, which showed me how much he was loved. During the first two hours of the service, anyone who wanted to stand up and say something about Emmanuel was allowed to. There were a vast number of people who stood and spoke about him, all saying nice things about growing up with him, going to church with him, co-workers speaking highly of him, etc.

As I sat back and watched, I had to admit how enlightening this was. It was most impressive to see that a man as quiet as Emmanuel, had such a positive and profound impact on so many people. What wonderful memories and an awesome legacy that he left behind.

Since attending his funeral, I have given a lot of thought about the events that took place that day: the enormous crowd of people; the beautifully kind things that were said; the pulling together by family, friends, and co-workers. I began to think about how I want to be remembered when I die. Obviously, I thought I'd like to be remembered as well as Emmanuel, but my thoughts went further. I started thinking about who might attend my funeral. I imagined what kinds of things my family, friends, and co-workers might say about me.

I'm currently 43 years old, and I hope to have a lot of time left here on earth, but anything could happen. The one thing that comes to mind every time I think on this subject is I want to be remembered for helping others. I want the Tar-Billy Cruisers campground to be a symbol of this. I want my family to be proud of how they raised me and for teaching me how to treat and respect my friends. I want my friends to be proud to have known me, and I want them to feel like they are as much kin to me as my blood relatives. Should I stay in management, I want people who have worked for me to show up and be able to honestly say I was one heck of a person to work for. I want them to say I was fair, consistent, and most of all as helpful as I could be when I could be.

Also, I want this book to be a symbol of making a difference in people's lives. My goal has been to write something that the everyday middle class, hard-working person could relate to. I want this to be a symbol of my family's love and support that they have shown me throughout the years. Most of all, I want my children to be proud of their daddy's accomplishments, proud that he would dream all he could dream and pursue every dream with the passion most people only dream about.

All of these thoughts originated from one funeral. If that funeral had this much effect on me, imagine the effect it had on the rest of the crowd that was there that day. Isn't it cool that one person could change so many lives? The more thought I give this, the more I hope my life is changing in a way that I can be remembered as well as Emmanuel.

Why do we do the things we do? How do you want to be remembered?

15

Dreams and Goals

Have you ever thought about dreams you've had that didn't come true and felt somewhat sad? Sometimes we build images in our mind for things to look a certain way, and when that image doesn't become reality, it can be disappointing. On the other hand, maybe there were some dreams that didn't come true and it turned out to be a blessing. We all dream, from the time we're just a few months old until we die, but isn't there something sad about a lost dream?

When we're young, it seems we have all the opportunity and time in the world to fulfill our dreams. Why are there some that we choose not to follow? I think some dreams can seem so big that we can't seem to get a grasp on how to pursue them, so we let them slide by. However, almost any dream can be accomplished if it is broken down into smaller goals, tasks, or steps that are more easily accomplished. This might be more difficult when we're younger, say just getting out of high school or college. But it is never too late. This is your life we are talking about that only you can change, and you only get one life.

Although I chose to follow one career, there were other careers I once dreamed about. Growing up, I remember thinking how neat it would be to become a traveling weatherman reporting on all of mother nature's fury. I never pursued this dream because it seemed like such an overwhelming task to accomplish. Now that I have some confidence in myself, I think I could have made it, and sometimes when I think about that it makes me sad. Yet, if I had followed that dream, there are things that I have now in my life that I might have missed out on. For instance, I most likely would not be a part of the Tar-Billys and probably wouldn't be writing this story. Thinking that way about it, I am thankful things worked out the way they did.

Most of you have heard the saying, "Find something you enjoy doing, figure out a way to make a living doing it, and you'll never work a day in your life." I think there is a lot of truth to that statement. I have always enjoyed being around the trucking industry. Even though I had other dreams, this dream was the one that meant the most to me, so I found a way to make it happen. It took me many years of challenges and several different positions to get to where I am, but I made it. Over the years, my mind allowed me to make the right decisions by breaking down my dream into smaller goals. Fueling trucks, washing trucks, moving trailers on the yard, and going back to driving school were the smaller goals I had to accomplish in order to get where I wanted to be. I paid attention to what was going on around me and took every opportunity I could to eventually reach my dream.

Though I had the dream of being a truck driver, and I never imagined myself doing anything else, things happened in my life that altered my dream. As my dream changed, and I decided to get into management, so did the smaller goals I had to set. I began making decisions based on that new dream. In addition to work, I am now trying to write a book, which has altered my mindset yet again. Another dream, another set of smaller goals that need to be set and accomplished to make the dream a reality. I am learning as I go. I did not realize there were so many decisions to be made in writing a book. Not only do you have to write the material, but you must decide on a title, an editor, a cover, and more. It can be quite overwhelming.

If you had told me when I was eighteen years old that I would be doing the things I am doing now, I wouldn't have believed it. Just like me, you can do the same. Don't give up on your dreams because you fear failure. Set small goals and work to accomplish each one. Remember that nothing is out of your reach if you want it badly enough. The only things you will regret in life are the things you do not try.

16

After Graduation

Ever since I got out of school, I wanted to finish this book. I put it off because I just didn't feel like I had an ending to my story. I knew I wanted to utilize my degrees, but I also knew there was not a lot of opportunity at Food Lion. Leaving would be a hard decision because I'd been there for so long and I was comfortable. At the same time, by staying, I felt as though I'd be settling for "good enough." Having come this far, I decided it was time to move on, and so I began looking around for other opportunities.

I did a lot of interviewing, but it was tough to find something that was the right fit for me. Many of the jobs I interviewed for were in other states, as there wasn't a lot of opportunity in my area for someone with my skill set. In March 2013, I got a job as Process Improvement Manager at a food service company. This worked out to be basically a fleet manager's position. Not long after I was hired, there was a new executive hired as a Senior Vice President by the name of Ron Banks. Ron was super to work for. In fact, I found out he and Rudy (from Food Lion) had come up through their careers together. I quickly realized they had a lot in common.

I learned so much from Ron during my time there. I learned you have to manage up and down in today's business world. This means having to guide those above you to create buy-in for where you are wanting to take the business, and once you have buy-in at the top, then you need to achieve buy-in for those that work for you. I also learned that everyone's a winner until they prove otherwise. Coming into an organization as a new manager and not knowing anyone at the company nor their history with the company, it's good practice to give everyone a chance to prove they can handle their responsibilities. I learned how to break big business down into small understandable parts and that little things make a huge difference to the bottom line. The most important lesson I learned is you cannot dream your way to success. In today's world, so many people want to end their day at 5:00 p.m., then go home and dream about where they want to be later in life. If you are trying to climb the corporate ladder, ending your day at 5:00 p.m. every day is probably not going to get you very far. It's nice to go home at 5:00 p.m., but those who really want to move up in their careers stay until that day's job is done and then prepare for the next day. It's not always fun, but it is essential to success. Turning those dreams into reality takes dedication.

Ron had about six direct reports. Most of us, including Ron, were willing to do whatever it took to get the job done. There were a lot of late nights, weekends, and very little sleep in this job. I found it so inspiring that Ron was willing to put out just as much effort as the rest of us. Ron told us he never slept, so to call if we needed anything. That was not just a saying, it was reality. Imagine a senior vice president working on a project or issue at two in the morning. Not all executives are willing to help employees after hours.

At one of my jobs, we had an issue with a third party company in the wee hours of the morning. One of the vice presidents for the third party company ended up on a conference call and I heard him make the statement, "How is this my problem?". He was upset because he'd been woken up. Don't get me wrong, nobody likes to get called in the middle of the night. However, executives of large companies are normally under a responsibility to do everything in their power legally and ethically to get the customer up and running as quickly as possible. In fact, if a customer has an issue, it is everyone's responsibility to get that customer's issue resolved.

Ron wasn't at all like that vice president. Always willing to help customers and anyone in the company, Ron made himself available twenty-four hours a day, seven days a week. This was fortunate for us because we had so much going on there was no way to get it done in an eight-, ten-, or twelve-hour day.

By working so many hours, this new job allowed me to do many new and interesting things. I learned how to spec out a fleet, negotiate contracts, and manage vendors. These were much different tasks from what I'd done before like managing drivers and getting trailer-loads of groceries out of the gate. Ron believed in me and was willing to help me with things I didn't understand. That meant a lot to me.

I spent about fourteen months in this position. I worked hard and our efforts saved the company a lot of money. However, I wasn't comfortable with some of the decisions being made above Ron in other parts of the company and decided to leave for a position with a leasing company in May 2014 to be a Safety Manager. This job required a lot of travel, but I was okay with that. Wanting to move up, it was essential for me to learn more about the safety side of things. This job, however, came with a lot of politics, and I don't do well with politics. I accomplished my goal of learning the safety side of things, but the job was short lived. After about nine months, I was laid off.

For the first time in my adult life, I was unemployed.

Though I worried about what I would do and how this would impact my family, I knew that with my experience and education I'd find another job. My wife reminded me I had been going at it hard for many years. Fortunately, we were in a good enough place financially that I didn't need to take the next job offer that came along. I had time to look around to find something that was a good fit for me. I spent about four months at home and then went back to driving a truck part time for about seven months for Larry Barbour.

Larry and his wife Joann were good to me while I was working for them. They allowed me to take off when I had to go to interviews. It was important for me to stay focused on finding the right fit. I interviewed with numerous companies and as most of you know, interviewing is not easy. You want to answer the questions right to be considered for the job, but if you disagree with a question, you need to be able to explain yourself in a way to get the company to consider your ideas. Some companies wanted me to relocate for a job with tremendous responsibilities for very little pay. Some companies I visited had run down facilities that I didn't want to take on. Other companies just didn't seem open to change. I knew somewhere out there was a company that would love to have someone like me on their payroll. I knew I would eventually find the company that would complete my story so I could finish my book.

I interviewed three times for a job with a company called Associated Asphalt in Roanoke, Va. I did the first interview over the phone in the parking lot of a concrete plant while driving a truck for Larry. During this interview with the Director of Sales and Logistics, Danny Moran asked me how I would go about finding new drivers. I explained to Danny it would depend on what kind of package the company had to offer a driver. I asked questions like, how do the drivers get paid, hourly or by the mile? Are drivers home every night? Do the drivers work a lot of weekends? Before I answered his question, I had to understand more about their program. Most importantly, I wanted to know why they didn't have drivers coming to them for jobs.

I explained to Danny if a company has a good enough package, they don't need to go looking for drivers, as word on the street gets out and drivers come looking to drive for a company with a good package. I explained that in the world I came from, referrals were your best recruits most of the time. I told him it doesn't hurt to advertise, but advertising locally will attract local drivers, rather than regional or national ones.

We talked for quite a bit. When I got off the phone and got back on the road, I remember thinking I probably blew that interview because I answered questions with questions. However, I was called back for two more interviews, both of them on-site in Roanoke. I interviewed with the President, CFO, VP, HR Manager, and Safety Manager. I went through these interviews the same as I had with Danny. When asked a question that didn't have a black and white answer, I would ask them a question to understand more about the company's perspective and what they were looking for before I answered.

I'm guessing the interview committee liked what I had to say, because I started work on February 8, 2016 as their Senior Transportation Manager. This is a small company that I have learned has lots of opportunity, great people, and a small company culture that cares about its workers. My fellow employees and I are treated extremely well here. I am at a point where I feel that all the challenges, lessons, late nights, and loss of sleep have finally paid off.

17

Success

There's no one single description of success because success can be many different things depending on the person or even just the situation. Success for me is making a difference in other people's lives. Even though I feel like I've made a difference in many people's lives already, I still don't feel successful. I went back to school and got two degrees, worked on and negotiated multi-million dollar deals, yet I always want to do more. This is the exact reason this book was written. Maybe, in some small way, it will make a difference for those that read it.

I was fortunate enough to attend the 2013 International Food Distribution Association (IFDA) Convention in Orlando, Florida. While I was there, I listened to two motivational speakers that I really enjoyed, and I can still remember the speech each one of them gave. To this day, I'm inspired by what I heard and would like to be able to give a speech like that one day. Both individuals told stories of their success. One story was about a person who took a cab ride to a completely new level. The other was about college athletes who are in the spotlight all the time.

One thing I've noticed about success is that it is all about the decisions you make. To be successful, you must first answer three questions: *What would success look like for you?, Are you willing to do what it takes to reach your goal?*, and *Are you willing to roll up your sleeves and dive into any project?*

The first one is fairly simple. If you don't know where you want to go, how will you know how to get there? You must envision what success looks like to you. Once you do that, you will begin thinking in a way that will lead you to success, that is, if you want it badly enough. When I went back to school, I knew I wanted to be a Transportation Manager, and I knew a degree would help me to successfully accomplish my goal. Therefore, going back to school was part of my path toward my success.

Next, *Are you willing to do what it takes to reach your goal?* I can tell you from experience doing what it takes doesn't always come easy. I've witnessed many people who want to reach their goal, but when they find out how hard it is, they stop putting in the effort to pursue it because they feel the work is overwhelming. Remember, you have to take it in small steps, as it is not going to happen overnight or easily. In my particular case, the hours were brutal, I was always tired, and I lost so much time with my family and friends. But those were the sacrifices I had to make to be successful.

Finally, *Are you willing to roll up your sleeves and dive into any project?* A lot of people shy away from projects because they don't understand them. I have been approached with many projects throughout my career that I didn't understand. For example, I had asked our company to acquire a system to track the maintenance on our trucks at Associated Asphalt. We looked at a system, but couldn't get together on the price. The IT department asked me what I wanted this system to do. I briefly explained how it would track the maintenance intervals for each piece of equipment, alerting the managers when maintenance is required, thus giving us a way of tracking costs associated with maintenance and repairs. The

IT department told me to write it up and they would program it. My response was, "I don't know how to even start writing something of that magnitude," which is unlike me, because I am not scared of a challenge. The IT department again said, "You write it and we will program it."

I agreed to do this, all the while not having a clue where to begin. I had never written anything to be programmed. After a couple weeks of thinking about it, I started out with a blank Word document and typed in the basics of what I wanted the system to do. Once I got the basics in, then I had a clearer picture and started adding in enhancements, which led to more enhancements. Long story short, that program is being used today and is working great. I almost walked away from a project that was presented to me because I didn't know how to do it, and that scared me. In reality I knew more than I thought I did. What's more, my co-workers believed in me more than I believed in myself.

Another move toward being successful is to surround yourself with as many people as you can that are already involved in the area of your interest. You don't think Dale Earnhardt became a famous racecar driver by hanging out with accountants all day do you? No, he hung out at the racetrack with drivers, mechanics, and car owners. He learned the business from the ground up, which is very important. Many people have reached the top without learning the entire business, and then when they find themselves in a situation that they haven't encountered before, they don't know what to do. It's crucial to learn all the small things before you get to a role of making big decisions..

In my case, I had people like Rudy, Ron, and Danny to guide me. These guys knew the business from the bottom up because they had already come up through the ranks, like me. When I didn't understand something, they were willing to take the time to explain it to me. Rudy asked me one time what I wanted to do when I got out of school. I immediately answered that I wanted his job. Without hesitation, Rudy said, "I will help you if that's what you want to do." A lot of managers might have felt threatened by my statement, but not Rudy. He wanted to move up just as I did. He also knew the more successful I was in my role as a supervisor, the more successful he would be as a manager.

Moving toward success isn't just about listening and following along with everything you are told. One thing I have learned in this business is that no one person has all the answers. Even CEOs need guidance from their staff from time to time. Working with Ron, Rudy, and Danny, I felt comfortable to disagree and offer my opinion. They appreciated me speaking up and many times went along with my idea. Danny told me one time, "I didn't hire you to tell me what I want to hear, I hired you to help me run this business." I also believe that listening creates understanding. If you listen well and understand what is going on in your workplace, you will be able to share your perspective and others will listen and respect what you have to say.

A perfect example of success outside the workplace is the development of The Tar-Billy Cruisers' campground. Although we were all friends and family, we were still strangers to a new adventure. We knew we wanted a place in the mountains to call our own, but we were not clear as to how to go about it. As soon as the property was purchased, we immediately started exchanging ideas on how we thought the building should be done and how we wanted it to look when it was finished. There were so many different ideas, and we didn't know which one would be best, but we stayed committed to our goal-having a place of our own in the mountains.

As time went on, we prioritized what needed to be

done. Then as each task came up, everyone had a chance to voice his or her opinion on it. Being the link between North Carolina and West Virginia, I was the one who often had conversations with each individual. Once I was done gathering information, I'd make a decision based on what the majority wanted to do. Everyone understood that the majority ruled and went along with the final decision.

As each decision was made, each person was willing to do his or her part to complete the task. This was not always fun, in fact it was a lot of hard work. The Tar-Billy Cruisers had challenges to overcome. We all had to find time to make what was for some a three-hundred mile trip to the campground. We each had personal finances to consider in deciding whether we could afford the trip. We'd work from daylight to dark for three days straight for no compensation other than knowing we were getting closer to our goal. We all had to voice our opinions respectfully so as not to upset our friendships. I found it amazing that every time we went to work on the property, everyone seemed to find a way to make the trip so they could help. It was not one person's, or two people's efforts. For about four years everyone was willing to do whatever it took to accomplish our goal. It took everyone stepping out of our comfort zones and working toward the same goal as a team to reach success. Success that resulted in a place in the mountains that we could call our own.

18

Goals are Met . . . Now What?

After getting the job with Associated Asphalt, my goals up to this point were accomplished. The campground was done, I had finished school, and I'd obtained the job I wanted. The next thing to do was get my family moved from North Carolina to Virginia and finish this book, but getting my family moved was the most important, so the book had to wait.

Making a big move was something I had never done in my adult life. There were so many things to consider like how the move would affect the kids, finding a place to live, Julie finding work that would be accommodating to my busy schedule, and more. Finding a place to live was the hardest. After looking at houses and weighing out the options, we decided we would purchase a piece of property and build a house. I had heard horror stories of how aggravating the process was to build a house along with the marital issues it can create. Let me tell you first hand, they are all true.

The first thing we had to do was to find a builder. We looked at different builders and finally landed on one that was supposed to be the number one builder in the Roanoke Valley. Then we had to decide on the type of house we wanted built. The builder we chose had several different designs that they built, so we were able to pick from those designs, which was the easy part. Next we had to spec out the house to decide every little detail. The floor plan had to be determined, the colors, the wood used for the cabinets, the carpet, the windows, the location of the electrical box, the size of the hot water heater, and the list goes on. To put it into perspective, if you stick-build a house, then you have to decide every little detail of what goes on or in that house, from the shingles to the basement and even where your well and septic are located in the yard. I let Julie pick everything out.

Once all the decisions were made, we had to deal with the builders and contractors and weather. The majority of the building took place in 2018, and it rained what seemed like every other day. This created delay, but it wasn't too upsetting because you can't fight mother nature. The contractors on the other hand were an entirely different story. They wouldn't always show up, or they would show up late or leave early. Some things were done when they left, others weren't or were not right, so they would have to come back. The contract was written so that money was paid out to the contractor as the building process reached certain milestones. This sounds good in theory, but the contractor didn't always want to play by the rules of the contract. There were times when they wanted to be paid before the work was done. If you made any changes to the agreed upon spec, then you had to pay for those as you went.

In our situation, and just one example of many, the supervisor for the contractor didn't show up on the day of the initial meeting at the property to go over where to put the house. This created issues right out of the gate. The day they came to start digging the foundation, I was in South Carolina working and Julie was in North Carolina. The contractor supervisor called me and said he was sorry he wasn't there for the initial meeting, but we needed to consider flipping our house so that the garage would be on the left side and the bedrooms on the right side if you are looking at the front of the house. He explained that by doing this it would make our garage easier to access due to the slope of the ground. What he said made sense, having never built a house before, we hadn't thought about it from that perspective. At the end of the day, he was right, so we stopped the ground breaking. We had to go back to the specs and have a new floor plan drawn with the same house flipped before they could start.

Once the new floor plan was done, ground breaking began, but the new plan created other issues. We had originally planned for stone to go across the bottom back of the house because it would be exposed, and the rest of the house would be at ground level. By flipping the house, the left side of the house was now six feet from the ground to the vinyl siding and the front was now somewhat exposed. Logically, it wouldn't look right now with stone just across the back, so we decided to go with stone all the way around. This cost us an extra $10,000 for this one change, but that isn't the end of it.

The wall going on the left side was the wall for our basement. As the contractors were framing the wall to be poured with concrete, I happened to drop in. I noticed as I looked at the framing that the wall was going to look odd if we didn't put any windows in it, plus a window or two would allow more light into the basement. I called Julie and asked her about it. She was adamant that it didn't need windows. Though I didn't agree and we had words over it, I went along with her decision. A few days later, Julie came up from North Carolina and we went to the build site. The contractors were working and almost done with the framing job. We weren't there for ten minutes when Julie comes to me and says that we need to add windows on the left side. I am not going to lie, this did not sit well with me. In her defense, it is very hard to picture every little detail in your mind until you see it playing out, so I understood that it was frustrating for her too. Inevitably, I went back to the framers and asked them to go back to that left side and add in two more windows, but that still isn't the end of it.

Eventually the time came to put the stone up. We paid the extra money up front to have the stone go all the way around the house. The contractor that was putting the stone up was only doing very little at a time. Before he was done, the builder wanted to collect the money for that phase being complete. I explained to him it wasn't complete and he tried to tell me what he was asking for was the extra stone to go all the way around the house. I corrected him by showing him we had already paid that money. That builder and I argued about this for two weeks. I explained to him we had to follow the terms of the contract as it was put in place to protect him as the builder and us as the home owners. He finally got it done, and he finally got paid and moved on to the next phase, but what a fiasco!

Once the house was finished, the builder was paid in full and I was told they would come back in a year to fix anything we may find after we moved in that may have been missed during final inspection or that happened as a result of the house settling. We had it in writing that the house was under warranty for fifteen years, so I am thinking all is good, but I was wrong. Six months after our house was built, the builder went out of business. This meant they would not be coming back at the end of the first year, and my warranty wasn't any good because the builder didn't file the proper paperwork. But I was one of the lucky ones. That builder left dozens of homes he was building incomplete, which left dozens of families in a mess. Also, he left dozens of contractors unpaid. I understood after all this went down why he wanted his money early. He was floating his bills.

At any rate, we moved into our new home in October of 2018. It took a little over a year to get settled into our new home and community. Once we were settled, I decided this book needed to be done, so I started working on it again.

As for me and my future, who knows what it holds. The reality is that I'm not sure what I want to do from here. I've spent many years working many hours to get to where I am. I've learned that success comes with a price. I have finally found a company and a job that has some great people, a decent schedule, good pay, and favorable benefits. I have the right processes and procedures in place so that I don't have to work 20 hours a day anymore. I am at a point now where I can spend time with my friends and family. It's a great place to be, but is it enough?

Giving this a lot of thought, I continue to weigh my options. Maybe because there are times when I still feel that there is something more out there waiting for me. The fact that I feel like I have made a difference to so many encourages me to continue to pursue even greater dreams. The bottom line is that I am at a point in my life where I am comfortable. Considering that I have reached my goals and dreams, if I remain where I am, will I be settling for "good enough?" Should I continue to try to better myself in roles that I believe are helping others? Most days, I feel like I've got it in me to be a part of something much bigger. Therefore, let's see where this thing goes.

19

What I Have Learned and Some Advice

I got into management in 2005 to put myself in a position to make a difference. Over the course of the last 15 years, I have learned so much about management, people, and business. Before closing this book, I want to highlight some points that are relative to this book and my story.

I found out very quickly that only your true friends can really be trusted. I have always been a true believer in the fact that there are certain lines you don't cross if you really consider someone your friend. I think this stands true with friends we make throughout our entire life from grade school to our elderly years. I had some friends in school that are still my friends and others that I had to part ways with because they didn't know the true meaning of friendship. The Tar-Billys have never backed me in a corner. However, after getting into management, I have had drivers that I considered friends try to use our friendship as a way to get me to change things to benefit them. In management, decisions aren't based on what will help one person, but what will help the majority. Friendship has to be set aside in the business world.

Time can be a struggle. I mentioned how much time I spent in school and working two jobs. I am not putting in those kinds of hours on a regular basis now, but managing multiple facilities does require a lot of time. Being able to make a positive difference somewhere other than work is tough, because at the end of each day and week, you are worn out. Many times my mind is just mush at the end of the day. I don't feel like going anywhere or doing anything. When I am traveling I sit at the hotel, have a mixed drink or two, and spend time talking to my family and friends on the phone because I don't feel like going anywhere. As I look back, twenty some years ago working two jobs, I could go twenty hours a day without too much issue. Now, I can still put more hours in at work than most young people, but it takes me a little more time to get over it than it used to.

Another thing I've learned is understanding creates calmness. When I was a driver, I would get so upset because I couldn't figure out why management did some things that appeared really dumb. Once in management, I began to understand that many of the things that seemed dumb to me as a driver were not as dumb as they appeared. However, I also found that some things were just as dumb as they appeared to be. When I explained to employees why things were done a certain way some of their disgruntlement went away. I've tried to be a manager who takes the time to explain things to employees because I remember being in their shoes and thinking their same thoughts. As for the things that were as dumb as they appeared, they were my job to change. After all, that is why I got into management.

Speaking of change, I've learned that at any level of management you are expected to be an agent of change. Doing this requires you to manage up, down, and even side to side. If something needs changing, it is up to you to get your boss to see the value in making that change. You may need to present your ideas more than once or in different ways. You may need to get your peers involved by first making them see the value of your ideas. Once they are sold, they can be instrumental in helping you to persuade your boss. This can be a long process and it is crucial to be respectful through the entire process. Once you have managed up, you manage down by letting those under you know the outcome. No matter the outcome, most employees will be appreciative that you tried to make a positive change and that you are willing to get in front of them with that information.

Employees who are unhappy in the workplace sometimes don't realize how their disgruntlement affects their co-workers. Most people want to come to work, make a decent salary, and go home. Many people will settle for a lower salary to work in a positive environment where they feel respected by both their peers and management. Nobody wants to work in a place where workers are negative or on edge all the time. Employees don't want to listen to their coworkers spewing negativities and smart remarks, but sometimes they won't say anything to stifle the negative comments. Unfortunately, negativity spreads like a cancer. Employees get tired of hearing it and start complaining to their manager. Some decide to leave all together. The majority of the time, those spewing negativity don't realize their audience is only listening to them because they are too nice to say anything. Negative people are often on an island by themselves, but do not realize it.

When I was growing up, my dad would stay on me about how I talked. He was not talking about my speech, just the way I would come across as a smart ass and a know-it-all. He would always remind me to watch my grandfather and how slow he talked so he could choose his words and his tone wisely. As a teenager, I got tired of hearing him fuss at me because I didn't think I was doing anything wrong. Now years later, I am so glad he stayed on me about it.

Taking an issue to your manager respectfully and with an open mind lets him or her know that you truly want to resolve the issue and not just ruin everyone else's day. They'll be more willing to help you because, after all, how can they explain anything to you if you already have all the answers?

As hard as you might try, sometimes it is difficult to make a difference, despite how badly you might want to. Some people are disgruntled because of companies they've worked for in the past and their attitude carries over into the work they do for you, even though it is not a result of anything you have done.

After being in management a while, I became very discouraged in trying to help others. I found myself in a place where I was trying to satisfy others rather than help them. I got to a point where some people expected it and would be demanding until it was almost insubordination. I received comments that were sarcastic accompanied with foul language and smart remarks. Being treated this way has sometimes been enough to make me think about quitting, but I can't for these three reasons:

1. There are some who truly appreciate what you do for them. A sincere thank you from someone is the best compensation in the world. As long as I am doing what is right and some folks appreciate it, I have to continue on.
2. Part of the challenge in management is figuring out people, and I don't walk away from a challenge.
3. As a manager, I have to be tougher than my subordinates. My job is to listen and make decisions based on what I have heard to make a positive difference for the company and the employees. Anytime you listen to disgruntled employees, you'd better have some thick skin or they will bury you. I had a manager tell me one time,

"You let drivers talk down to you too much." My response was, "Being the senior manager, I can change the conversation anytime I want, but if I let them talk then I will eventually get to the root of the problem." In management, it is not about ego or winning every conversation, it is about doing what is right for the business and the employees, which requires thick skin.

Management is all about understanding people and communicating with them. Listening is your most important asset and often your toughest challenge. Sometimes when listening to others it can seem that they are attacking you as a person and in some cases, they may be. Being able to bite your tongue and let someone talk is as important as it is hard, but hearing someone out can be crucial to getting to the root of the problem. Once you have a better understanding of the problem and can respond appropriately. Being able to speak to your audience in a way they can understand can be as challenging as listening. Some will not like what you have to say, but most will appreciate your honesty no matter the message you are conveying.

As a manager, I realize that I am responsible for setting the tone in the workplace. I play a big part in creating the perception employees have about me and the culture of the company. This in turn can determine how much pride they take in their jobs. If employees perceive that I don't care about the success of the business, then it's likely they will demonstrate the same attitude. Good managers continually reevaluate their business and try to make it better all the time. It is an ongoing process because the work environment can change quickly.

Finally, I would like to offer some friendly advice to truck drivers, blue-collar workers in their various roles, and owners/managers.

Truck Drivers:

1. **Safety should be your number one priority every** day at all times. Everything you do in or around your truck will be under tremendous scrutiny should an accident occur. Be sure you adhere to safety precautions and procedures. No matter the delivery schedule, I advise you not to speed, make sure you aren't following too closely, keep an eye on your surroundings at all times, and if you get sleepy, stop the truck and rest your eyes for a bit. Some companies may frown on this, but a good company would much rather explain to a customer why you were thirty minutes late to a delivery than face a lawsuit because you were speeding or fell asleep trying to get there and had an accident.

2. **Do good pre-trip and post-trip inspections.** If something falls off the truck while you are the operator, it is your fault. Take the time to look everything over and report anything you find wrong so it can be repaired before the equipment is taken back out on the road.

3. **Get a license without automatic transmission re**striction. Although automatics are taking over, manuals will still be around for quite a few more years. A license without a restriction gives you an edge when applying for jobs and more opportunities within a company.

4. **Understand how to operate the truck efficiently.** As company operating costs continue to rise, fuel efficiency is becoming more and more important. One-tenth of a mile better fuel economy makes a huge difference in a fleet running ten million miles per year.

5.   **Know the law and how it applies to different parts** of the industry by familiarizing yourself with the guidelines in the FMCSA green regulations book. The book can be confusing, but your manager will be able to help you understand things that may seem unclear.

6.   **Protect your license by staying away from drugs** and alcohol. This will ruin you faster than anything. So many drivers have lost their license because they had one or two drinks and thought they were fine to drive. Other drivers have taken someone else's prescribed medication so they wouldn't need to make a trip to the doctor, and then they got popped for a random check.

All Workers:

1.   **Show up every day on time and ready to work.**

2.   **Once you get to work, plan to stay as long as you** are needed. Things come up from time to time when you might need to leave a little early, but this should be the exception, not the rule. This will go a long way with your manager because it really shows you want to work.

3.   **Know what you are signing up for. I have seen so** many people take jobs and within one to three weeks they leave because before they were hired they didn't understand the hours, the process, physical demands, etc.

4.   **Listen and learn everything you can. If you are** happy with your position and don't want to move anywhere else, that is fine, but you still need to listen and learn about the entire process. Who knows, one day your position may go away. If that happens, wouldn't it be nice to be able to simply transfer to another job because you already understand the process?

5.   **You cannot get your work done if you are looking** at your phone every two minutes. Make sure your friends

and family know your work schedule so they will know when not to call or text you and when they might expect a call or text back from you during a break. If an employer is paying you for so many hours a day, that employer expects you to be working during those hours.

6. **Volunteer for weekends and holidays when you** can. Nobody likes working weekends and holidays including me, but this shows the company you are a team player and willing to go the extra mile. Good managers will notice and keep you in mind for promotions when they open up.

7. **Talk to your manager, not your co-workers, about** your concerns. Your manager has the power to change things if necessary, not your co-workers. A good manager will appreciate you bringing your concerns to him/her and will take the time to listen and explain why certain things can't be changed, or make changes where he/she can.

Managers and Owners: This is manager 101 stuff, but just a few reminders.

1. **Always take the time to listen to your employees.** This can be hard especially if they are a little wound up, but it's important that you allow them the freedom to voice their concerns.

2. **Know that you don't have to give employees an** answer right away. It is perfectly fine to let them know when you don't have an answer and that you will get back to them. Just be sure that you follow through. It was important enough for them to bring it to you, it should be important enough for you to get back to them.

3. **Though you can't always give employees the an-** swer they want to hear, most will appreciate the fact that

you got back to them and the fact that you've been honest with them.

4. **Treat everyone with respect. Don't play favorites.** It creates a negative work environment.

5. **As a manager, it is your job to serve. Be willing to** adjust your hours to make yourself available to your employees.

6. **Last but not least, it is a tough spot to be in when** trying to find the happy medium between what is right for the company and what is right for the employees, but that is your job. This can make for some pretty tough conversations, but being able to listen and communicate respectfully with upper management, your peers, and your employees will make these tough conversations much easier.

Finally, remember that no matter what life throws at you, keep on trucking!

CPSIA information can be obtained
at www.ICGtesting.com
Printed in the USA
LVHW050307090622
720760LV00015B/1303